The Vast Venus Conspiracy

Volume IV of the Venus Rising Series:
A Concise History of the Second Planet

Ladies Columba (L) and Aurora (R) beam down to attend a lecture of the Cosmic Ray in Northwestern Pennsylvania.

Drawing of Lady Orda made by Dr. George Hunt Williamson based on his observations of her emergence from a Venusian scout ship on 20 November 1952 at Desert Center, California.

Dr. Raymond Andrew Keller, II,
a.k.a. "Cosmic Ray"

Headline Books, Inc.
Terra Alta, WV

The Vast Venus Conspiracy
Volume IV of the Venus Rising Series: A Concise History of the Second Planet

by Dr. Raymond Andrew Keller, II

To order additional copies of this book or for book publishing information, or to contact the author:

Headline Books, Inc.
P.O. Box 52
Terra Alta, WV 26764
www.headlinebooks.com

Tel: 304-789-3001
Email: mybook@headlinebooks.com

ISBN 13: 9781951556211

Library of Congress Control Number: 2020939984

PRINTED IN THE UNITED STATES OF AMERICA

This book is dedicated to all those emulating our brothers and sisters of Venus, working to build a paradise here on Earth.

Contents

Introduction by Robert Potter of the Promise Revealed 5
Chapter 1: On the Book of Abraham and the Plurality of Gods 11
Chapter 2: The Vast Venus Conspiracy 21
Chapter 3: The Kenneth Arnold Files 34
Chapter 4: Venusian Spaceships Are Landing! 53
Chapter 5: The Truth that Was Out There: Long John Nebel's Fight against the Censorship of Flying Saucer Reports 68
Chapter 6: Dominick Lucchesi Meets the "Space Girl" 81
Chapter 7: Activities of the North Jersey U.F.O. Group 104
Chapter 8: Dr. James E. McDonald and the Extraterrestrial Hypothesis 117
Chapter 9: The Moon is a Venusian Colony 129
Acknowledgements 140
Index 141

Introduction

Dear Friends of Venus,

It is my great joy, privilege and honor to write the introduction to this new book that you are reading. The reason is that I am so very excited for as many people as possible to learn of the great soul known as Dr. Raymond Andrew Keller, II.

I personally learned about Raymond through Frank Chille. Frank is an old friend of mine from 1978 who is a wonderful and enthusiastic brother with vast knowledge of the Space Brothers and Sisters that serve our Mother Earth. Frank and I spent many hours together in association with a famous contactee named Gabriel Green who lived in Yucca Valley, California. Like you, I am an earnest and diligent seeker of truth and rejoice whenever I find an authentic source of information on any subject. Not unlike Raymond, I can say my life has been a calling towards a true gnosis of our Space Family and our relationship with them.

Celestial Brothers: "Cosmic Ray" Keller (left) with Rob Potter at Mt. Shasta, CA, "From Venus with Love" world conference, 27-29 July 2018.

November 2017 sees Cosmic Ray enter into my life. After a series of amazing phone calls with the Coz, I realized the spiritual knowledge he shared with me was unparalleled. Many contactees are often recognized as intelligent and intuitively adept, but I understood Raymond was in class all by himself.

I also knew Raymond was a very special soul by the warmth he always exuded. I have analyzed many other contactees and feel I have a good understanding of who is for real and those who are struggling to define their contact experience. Raymond is a well-adjusted contactee who is fulfilling a great purpose by writing these books.

In the beginning of our association, my skeptical nature and judgmental character were being put to the test by my conversations with Raymond. However, he not only expanded my knowledge of the extraterrestrials and their mission to Earth, he also helped me to realize many things about myself. The first was that the universe is NOT always what we think it is. What we Earth people think we actually know about space and the scientific facts and physics of space travel is really a pittance. When we compare ourselves- our culture- to the 3 billion year cultural history of the Venusian inhabitants, we are surely infants in cosmic knowledge.

I realized I was extremely blessed when I had this knowing feeling that I had found a loving teacher of light in Raymond. It was soon after that I began a series of interviews and conversations with my favorite "Egghead of UFO Research." I say this with great adoration of my dear friend whom I openly consider to be a genius when it comes to writing.

His ***Venus Rising Trilogy***, a concise history of the second planet, is by far the most well-researched book on the history of the planet Venus ever written. Never before has such a compendium of information been placed into the public domain.

"Coz," as his close friends call him, is a dear brother and a true master in the humblest sense of the word. Frank Chille, Raymond and I, all considered Gabriel Green a true mentor in our quest for light and understanding on the road to truth.

We can all attest to the magnificence of Gabe's knowledge. Gabe would share his experiences and always was generous and kind to all of us. Gabe freely showered a tremendous amount of information on all who would knock on his door seeking answers.

Because the Space Family was monitoring the visitors who came to Gabriel's house in the California desert, they often provided unique experiences for the disciples under his tutelage. These experiences were designed to let the students know the Space Family was real. Furthermore, we all realized the Brothers were watching; and their technology that they used for this monitoring was being used responsibly. They would move things in the house, like a painting on the wall, to emphasize a point in the conversation. Sometimes lights would turn on and off as well as a TV in another room.

These were some of the many significant "phenomena"- type experiences at Gabe's house. For me, these also included being taken to a location where a spaceship landed in the desert not 30 feet from me. I also received a phone call from outer space after Gabriel called me once! This may sound a little far fetched for the average person, but I can assure you this was all very real.

I myself have been privileged like Cosmic Ray to have some physical contacts with Venusians and Pleiadian people. These experiences were very exciting and informative in many ways but are nothing like the physical contact experiences of Cosmic Ray.

Raymond was very fortunate indeed that Gabe introduced him to a woman named "Dolores Barrios," who at that time Raymond thought was a UFO researcher. However, at that time she was secretly residing on Venus and was appearing to many contactees to aid them in their missions to bring the truth to the people of the Earth.

This is the truth that Raymond and I are striving to share today. We wish for the people of Earth to rest assured that the peaceful mission of our Venusian cousins will someday be realized. I hope that soon we together as brothers and sisters will worship in the power of love as the Anointed One taught us nearly 2,000 years ago.

Raymond has listed his books as "magic realism" to be accepted by the public. Do not be fooled by these limiting words, which tend to have the reader considering this book series as works of fiction only. Raymond's knowledge of the Space Family is from first-hand experience. His experiences are beyond any magic possible by any Earth-based magician. These books are actually written from knowledge garnered from his personal contacts. He is by far one of the most important contactees of our time.

In fact, Raymond's narrative is more profound than a cursory examination of his books would allow. The trilogy to the date of this writing is more than a simple tome by a respected researcher. It must be fully understood and read with an open mind and a pure heart to plumb the depths of its amazing revelation.

Raymond has been thrust into the public eye since the age of 15 when he and a friend saw a space ship and their story was in the ***National Enquirer***. Raymond has been the author of numerous articles on extraterrestrial space ships.

Among his sundry talents and accomplishments, I can say he has created countless groups and newsletters studying flying saucers. He also seems to know more about almost every contactee and researcher that I have ever heard of and knows their contributions like the back of his hand. He also counts as friends many researchers who share with him special documents and evidence that are not so publically well known. He knows personally Dr. Leo Sprinkle, the late Dr. J. Allen Hynek and so many others, all with tremendous research libraries. Ray's research is painstaking and laborious.

When Raymond is done with a book, we are left with a finely polished jewel that reflects the deeper truths important to the real ongoing process I call "Interplanetary Cultural Exchange." When I find some information in one of his books that is special and query him, he will often downplay his experience. He is really just being shy and humble because he has been privileged to live on Venus for a two-and-a-half-months period between December 2012 and February 2013. This is not a joke. This is not a fantasy. This is a real contact experience that he has had and continues to enjoy to this day.

In the beginning or our association, I myself thought I was an open-minded person; but I found myself in a state of disbelief and wanting to challenge Raymond's honesty. In truth, I should have been checking my ego and what I thought to be real. His books are written in a sly way so as to cloak his vast contact experiences between the lines, so to speak.

This is particularly true in the first two books; ***Venus Rising*** and ***Rockets to Venus***. These books are filled with little-known facts. These books correct, chide and scold the establishment of the scientists, NASA, and most of the governments of the world that are knowing participants in this cover-up of the truth that we are openly being visited by benevolent friends from Venus and others within our own solar system and beyond. These cover-ups are vain attempts to dispatch the truth that the universe is teeming with life. Don't worry, though, for the truth has a way of making itself known despite mankind's stubborn insistence in shoving its proverbial head into the sand of doubt, even in the face of mountains of evidence.

In fact, I am encouraged to share with you Queen Orda's message that, "Venus and the Hierarchy of Light extends joyous greetings to the people of Earth. Venus is the highest manifestation love on the physical plane in the solar system." Read on, dear friends, to learn about Raymond's excellent adventure and wonderful experiences.

In Ray's third book, his fantastic research is filled with so many tidbits of little-known truth that the astute reader will be gratefully satisfied. This primary experience that he has enjoyed is one that you can read about in the third book of the trilogy titled, ***Cosmic Ray's Excellent Venus Adventure***.

Please get all of these books, if you can, as these are crucial to demystifying the Space Family and their mission to Earth. I also feel it is important for you all to know that Raymond is chosen to be a custodian of this hitherto-hidden knowledge because of his well-balanced personality. Raymond exhibits in his character a truly special development of the highest virtues. Like my other Venusian-contactee friends Dr. Frank Stranges, Luis Mostajo and even my "Little Venusian" friend who came from the fifth dimension, Omnec Onec, Raymond is a shining example of what a person should be. Cosmic Ray is honest, kind, humble and always thinking of others. He is always patient and never raises his voice or says anything bad about anybody.

He works serving those less fortunate and continues to volunteer countless hours to helping those who cannot help themselves due to age, financial condition and health challenges. We all could use his life of service as an example for us all to follow.

In the trilogy of books you will learn some of the following information:

1. Raymond was living in China when Dolores Barrios (a.k.a. Lady Orda) invited him to an "Ascension Party."
2. Raymond traveled in a "nimbus" to Tibet and then onto Venus via a mothership.
3. He watches spellbound as Lady Mazu, the Chinese Saint, ascends to the Great Central Sun.
4. His friend who invited him to Venus, Dolores Barrios, is announced the new Queen of Venus!
5. He meets with "wonderment and awe" the ascended master El Morya, the "Accidental Apostle" or "Lord Dysmas."
6. He soon receives permission from Morya and the newly-installed Queen Orda to view the Akashic Records. He does so despite the Chrono-Masters' objections.
7. He spends two-and-a-half months viewing the Earth's history and even enjoys glimpses of its future. In these forays, he learns previously unknown details about the Earth's relationship with Venus by means of a special viewing apparatus.
8. He sees all of his previous lifetimes, including his first incarnation as the Roman scribe and poet, Publius Vergilius Maro.
9. Finally, he actually travels back in time to 1954 with the current Queen of Venus, his friend Lady Orda.
10. Due to nuclear experiments of the 1950s, the bi- location technology of their time-travelling "nimbus" is disrupted by distortions in the tachyon field, thus leaving Raymond and the Queen literally lost in time!

I am sure all of this has blown your mind; so I will refrain from more seemingly "outlandish" tales. However, I suggest you buy all of these books as soon as possible to determine for yourself the veracity of these stories.

Nevertheless, I can promise that you will learn more about our amazing and vast universe and the Pleroma, filled as it is with various beings that inhabit the multi-dimensional planes of existence. The remaining knowledge Raymond has to share is so vast and covers so much information it is truly the eighth wonder of the world. Let's hope he can finish the other eight books that are waiting in his fertile mind to be shared with us all.

I wish to thank you all for reading this; and I hope you will forgive my extremely long introduction. I have recently returned from China with Raymond on a speaking tour and I have been able to know him better than ever. He is so full of love and has such a great sense of humor, that I have come to realize that it is my mission to reveal him for the "diamond" he is, hidden in the rough of today's world behind the curtain of confusion.

Please pause for a moment to try to grasp that the Venusian mission of peace is a spiritual one to connect us all to our authentic selves in an ongoing eternal revelation of truth. Look past the current sensationalist talk of disclosure and prognostications of those with little or no experience. Rather, we should look to the core of the Space Family's intent and their attempts to lift us up from our self-created quagmire of mental speculation, superstition and fear.

Please trust that we will assuredly eventually rise to the heights beyond hate and death and war to the glorious future that is awaiting us in the evolution of humankind to the stars and beyond. I will bid you "adieu" for now and wish to thank Raymond and Lady Orda for their confidence and support in me. The time they have taken to encourage me to go forward has provided a great bolstering to my path in life and faith towards establishing the presence of God in my own life.

Warm Regards, and Victory to the Light!
Rob Potter, Mt. Shasta, California
May 7, 2019

"Cosmic Ray" Keller, the Venus historian, and Omnec Onec, the Ambassador from Venus, shared recollections of our sister planet at the "From Venus With Love" conference at the foot of Mt. Shasta in Northern California, 27-29 July 2018.

Lady Columba (left) and Lady Aurora (right), were two emissaries dispatched by Queen Orda of Venus to attend the premier showing of Dr. Keller's second and third books in his *Venus Rising* series on 24 June 2017, coincidentally the 70th anniversary of flying saucers over the United States.

Chapter 1:
On the Book of Abraham and the Plurality of Gods

Above: "Council of the Gods" in the Galleria Borghese, Rome, Italy. In this chapter, Greco-Roman mythologist and Theosophist Dr. Raymond Keller, the author of the *Venus Rising Trilogy*, explains how the Mormon prophet Joseph Smith, Jr., imparted a Gnostic view of the universe. Presaging Erich von Däniken by more than 130 years, the visionary Smith provided key insights into the inhabitants of the celestial realms.

"I think all human beings have a godlike, divine power, only most of us don't tap into it."
—Ruby Dee (American actress and poet, 1922-2014)

While the *Book of Abraham* has never been considered as a scripture by the Reorganized Church of Jesus Christ of Latter Day Saints or its successor, the Community of Christ, it is credited as having been written by the prophet Joseph Smith, Jr., during the years of 1835-1842. As such, it has inestimable value to both the historian of church history and the theologian of restoration thought and the emerging religious consciousness of frontier America. Interestingly, the Church of Jesus Christ of Latter-day Saints, in Salt Lake City, Utah, did canonize the *Book of Abraham* as one of their sacred texts in 1880. For these reasons, Richard P. Howard, the historian of the Reorganized Church of Jesus Christ of Latter-day Saints from 1966 to 1994, headquartered in Independence, Missouri, has stated that, "These two factors alone make this subject a suitable matter for inquiry here."[1]

1 Richard P. Howard, *Restoration Scriptures: A Study of Their Textual Development*, 2nd edition (Independence, Missouri: Herald Publishing House, 1995), 193.

***Book of Abraham* History**

In the summer of 1835, an entrepreneur named Michael Chandler arrived at the church's headquarters in Kirtland, Ohio, with four mummies and multiple rolls of papyrus. Due in part to the exploits of the French emperor Napoleon Bonaparte, the antiquities unearthed in the catacombs of Egypt evoked quite a fascination throughout the Western world. Chandler capitalized on this interest by taking some of these appropriated Egyptian artifacts on a road show, charging visitors a fee to view them.[2]

Naturally, the arrival of these artifacts in the world center of Mormonism caused quite a stir. The Mormons themselves believed that the Native Americans scattered throughout the entire Western Hemisphere were descended from the ancient Israelites who, once they arrived in the Americas, split into two warring factions, the Nephites and the Lamanites. With the help of special optical and auditory aids given to him by an angel, the young prophet Smith was able to translate the golden plates he had dug up in the woods outside his Palmyra, New York, home, purportedly written originally in "Reformed Egyptian" into the *Book of Mormon* that we have today in the restoration churches. The enthusiastic members of Smith's new church were hoping that the discovery of the Egyptian papyri would shed new light and knowledge on the already existing scriptures found in the *Book of Mormon*. What they discovered, however, would have a much greater, yet unforeseen impact, significantly shaping the theology of the restoration churches and the religious movement that would one day attract millions upon millions more believers, clearly placing it in the Gnostic camp, whether the Mormon adherents and leadership, then or now, recognized this or not.

It was Antonio Lebolo, a former cavalryman in the Italian army, who oversaw some of the Egyptian excavations at the behest of Napoleon Bonaparte. In the conduct of his archaeological investigations, Lebolo pulled 11 mummies from a tomb not far from the ancient city of Thebes, whence he shipped the artifacts to Italy to be processed and catalogued. After his untimely death, however, Lebolo's Egyptian collection found its way to New York; and at some point the mummies and cryptic scrolls came into Chandler's custody.[3]

However, it should be noted that by the time the collection arrived in Kirtland, all but four of the mummies and several papyrus scrolls had already been sold. At an emergency meeting of the Presiding Elders convened at Kirtland, Ohio, a decision was reached that the remaining artifacts would be purchased by the church, to be turned over to their leader, Joseph Smith, Jr. Of course, Smith was delighted to take possession of the artifacts. And upon examining the papyri, the prophet noted that in the translation of some of the characters or hieroglyphics, "much to our joy we found that one of the scrolls contained the writings of Abraham."[4]

***Book of Abraham* on the Plurality of Gods**

The *Book of Abraham* has become the most controversial of latter-day scriptures insofar as it asserts the existence of many gods. And what is more, it maintains that the gods had not created the Earth *ex-nihilo*, or literally "out of nothing." These exalted beings accomplished

2 "Translation and Historicity of the *Book of Abraham*," author unspecified, *Church of Jesus Christ of Latter-day Saints, Intellectual Reserve, Inc*., 2014, https://www.lds.org/topics/translation-and-historicity-of-the-book-of-abraham?lang=eng (Accessed 19 April 2018).

3 H. D. Peterson, *Story of the Book of Abraham: Mummies, Manuscripts, and Mormonism* (Salt Lake City, Utah: Deseret Book, 1995), 36-85. See also Brian L. Smith interview by Philip R. Webb, "Mystery of the Mummies: An Update on the Joseph Smith Collection," *Religious Studies Center Newsletter*, vol. 20, no. 2 (2005): 1-5, for a detailed account on the disposition of the artifacts after their arrival in the United States to the present day.

4 *Joseph Smith History, 1838-1856*, vol. B-1, 596, available at jospehsmithpapers.org (Accessed 19 April 2018).

this creative process through the use of pre-existent materials, composed of pre-existent but eternal matter.[5]

Most restoration historians concur that Smith's move away from monotheism and towards polytheism took place during the period of 1838-39, when the prophet was held prisoner in Clay County, Missouri's Liberty Jail. While most of the *Book of Abraham* had already been translated, it had not yet been published. Smith felt confident in his translation of the papyri and noted that a time would come when nothing would be withheld from the saints; and they would know for themselves whether or not "there be one god or many gods."[6] This knowledge would become plainly manifest to all who diligently waited upon the word of the Lord. Brother Joseph did confide to the leadership of his church that he personally had visions of the One Eternal God presiding in a council with "all other gods before the world was."[7] What one can garner from this is that Smith clearly believed in the existence of One Eternal God; but it remains doubtful that he granted equal status to the lesser referenced deities. Thus we perceive a hierarchy of gods in the celestial realms.

While the historic leadership of the Reorganized Church of Jesus Christ of Latter Day Saints and the contemporary leadership of the Community of Christ has never taken the steps to canonize the *Book of Abraham* as their Salt Lake brethren have done, there have, nevertheless, been many in the ranks of these ecclesiastical organizations who have pushed for such recognition all along. The primary opposition to canonization has come from those holding to the more traditional Christian Trinitarian viewpoint with respect to the nature of God.

Theologian James R. White of the Christian Research Institute of Charlotte, North Carolina, has posited the following definition of the Trinity, one that he believes adequately communicates what needs to be said with the greatest clarity: "Within the one Being that is God, there exist eternally three coequal and coeternal Persons, namely, the Father, the Son, and the Holy Spirit. Each word of this definition is important. Each term carries weight and cannot be ignored. These few words present the three great foundations of the Christian doctrine of the Trinity: monotheism, the existence of three divine Persons, and the equality of those Persons."[8]

White has succeeded in expressing the traditional Christian view of the Trinity. This Trinitarian belief is also shared by the current priesthood hierarchy of the Community of Christ and forms an integral brick in the theological wall that separates this ecclesiastical organization from the larger restoration religious denomination in Salt Lake City, the Church of Jesus Christ of Latter-day Saints. This theological wall has largely come to be known as the "Mormon Boundary."

Here is the official Trinitarian doctrine espoused by the leadership in the Community of Christ and duly expressed as their basic belief about the nature of God:

"We believe in one living God who meets us in the testimony of Israel, is revealed in Jesus Christ, and moves through all creation as the Holy Spirit. We affirm the Trinity—God who is a community of three persons. All things that exist owe their being to God: mystery beyond

5 "Translation and Historicity"

6 Robert K. Ritner, *Joseph Smith Egyptian Papyri: A Complete Edition* (Salt Lake City, Utah: Signature Books), 30-33, 40.

7 Ibid., 40-41

8 James R. White, "Loving the Trinity," *Christian Research Journal*, Volume 21, Number 4 (July-August 1998), Charlotte, North Carolina, reprinted as *Statement DT 250* of the Christian Research Institute, Charlotte, North Carolina, 10 June 2009.

understanding and love beyond imagination. This God alone is worthy of our worship."[9]

In light of this clearly defined Trinitarian doctrinal statement, it surprised me to discover that such a strong belief in the unitary nature of God in three persons has not always been so emphasized in the history of the Community of Christ. Before this church began to call itself the Community of Christ in April 2001, it was widely known as the Reorganized Church of Jesus Christ of Latter Day Saints. Both the Reorganized Church of Jesus Christ of Latter-day Saints and the larger Salt Lake City church, commonly referred to as the Mormon Church, claim Joseph Smith, Jr., as their founding prophet. Smith restored the church to the Earth on 6 April 1830, incorporating it in Fayette, New York. The split between the two ecclesiastical organizations did not take place until 6 April 1860, in Amboy, Illinois, where many of those saints who did not follow the pioneering Apostle Brigham Young to Utah, reorganized the scattered remnant that went on to support the murdered prophet's son, Joseph Smith, III, to take the reigns as church president and carry on the gospel work initiated by his illustrious father.

Until the Community of Christ came about in 2001, with its emphasis on a more Christ-centered and Trinitarian doctrine, the members of the Reorganized Church of Jesus Christ of Latter Day Saints subscribed to a basic belief set as outlined in its *Epitome of Faith and Doctrine*.[10] It was originally delivered by the prophet Joseph Smith, Jr., with the first article declaring that, "We believe in God the Eternal Father, and in his Son Jesus Christ, and in the Holy Ghost."

Frankly, this statement is very nebulous. Since it was not overtly Trinitarian, it left a lot of room for conjecture and speculation. Was Smith referring to a belief in three gods or was an acceptance of the Trinity implied? From my personal experiences as a baptized member of the Reorganized Church, I would have to say that most members did not particularly care one way or another. Not so much concerned about the theological aspects of the religion, what they wanted most of all from their religion was the knowledge essential for establishing a personal relationship with Jesus. Subscribing to the notion that I would "rather see a sermon than hear one any day," I suppose that if I had to slot myself at some point along this theological continuum, I would side with the group that just wanted to see Jesus Christ at work in the lives of the saints and their respective communities.

As the Mormon Church also adopted a similar doctrinal statement, known as the *Articles of Faith*,[11] and based on the same *Times and Seasons* article by Smith cited below in the footnotes, it is no wonder that so much controversy emerged in the bodies of both churches as to just what the prophet Joseph Smith, Jr., really taught about the nature of God and the Trinity. The first article of the Mormon Church's version reads exactly the same as the first statement in the *Epitome of Faith*. Since the word "Trinity" does not even appear in the pages of the Bible, the topic of the plurality of gods was bound to arise sooner or later as one of the hot button issues among the saints in both restoration churches.

---

9 "Basic Beliefs," *Community of Christ*, 2018, http://www.cofchrist.org/basic-beliefs (Accessed 18 April 2018).

10 Joseph Smith, Jr., "Epitome of Faith and Doctrine," *Times and Seasons*, Volume 3, pages 709-710, Nauvoo, Illinois, 1942, as republished in "Our Beliefs," *Restored Gospel of Jesus Christ*, 2011, http://reorganizedchurch.org/beliefs.html (Accessed 18 April 2018).

11 Joseph Smith, Jr., "Articles of Faith," Church of Jesus Christ of Latter-day Saints, 2013, https://www.lds.org/scriptures/pgp/a-of-f/1 (Accessed 18 April 2018).

Canonization of Scripture in the Latter Days

1860 marked the first year for Joseph Smith, III, as president of the Reorganized Church. In that year, Isaac Sheen was serving as the editor of the church's official publication, the *Latter Day Saints' Herald*. The following is an extract from a groundbreaking article by Sheen, "A Plurality of Gods," that appeared in the December 186o edition of that monthly periodical:

> By the quotations of our Utah correspondent from the new translation of the Bible and from the *Book of Abraham*, it will be perceived that a plurality of Gods is a doctrine of those books. Although it is an unpopular doctrine, it is a doctrine of the common versions of the Bible...In *Genesis* 1:9 we read that "God said, Let us make man in our image, after our likeness." The words "us" and "our" signify more than one person, and those persons must have been Gods, for the work of creation belongs only to Deity... These scriptural evidences, concerning the order of the Kingdom in the exaltation of the sons of God, show that the revelations in the *New Testament* of the *Bible*, and in the *Book of Abraham*, concerning the gods, all harmonize together. When the doctrine came forth in these books, it became a stumbling block to some people. We hope that the evidence that we have presented on this subject will be advantageous in the removal of their stumbling block out of the way.[12]

From the archives of various publications that I have personally seen in the temple library of the Reorganized Church at Independence, Missouri, it is clear that there was an intense interest in and acceptance of the *Book of Abraham* and its advocacy for the doctrine of the plurality of gods. Howard, however, notes that the *Book of Abraham* continually declined in popularity among the saints of the reorganization throughout the waning years of the nineteenth century largely because Joseph Smith, III, the son of the assassinated prophet Joseph Smith, Jr., said very little about the book, one way or the other. In addition, the Latter-day Saints in Utah, under the leadership of their charismatic prophet Brigham Young (1801-1877), were constantly referencing and preaching from the book as if it were a scripture; and three years after Young's death had finally canonized the *Book of Abraham* to the status of a scripture in the church.

It was not until the administration of Lorenzo Snow, the fifth president of the Mormon Church, that the doctrine of the plurality of gods began to really gain more adherents. Lorenzo Snow, hailing from Mantua, Ohio, and being the brother to one of Joseph Smith, Junior's plural wives, Eliza R. Snow Smith, once spoke of our cosmic evolution, declaring that, "As man now is, God once was; and as God now is, man may be."

Of course, I was duly impressed by this statement. It was so in line with my Theosophical belief system. Since taking theology classes at the Community of Christ Seminary in Independence, Missouri, I revisited the history of this statement by Lorenzo Snow, and discovered that at the time he made it, in the spring of 1840, he was in Nauvoo, Illinois, and preparing to embark on a mission in the British Isles. Snow was visiting the home of his friend, HenryG. Sherwood, when he asked him if he could please explain a passage of scripture about man being created in the image and likeness of God. "While attentively listening to his explanation," President Snow later recalled, "the Spirit of the Lord rested mightily upon me—the eyes of my understanding were opened, and I saw as clear as the sun at noonday, with wonder and astonishment, the pathway of God and man. I formed the following couplet which expresses the revelation, as it was shown me, that being 'As man now is....'"

12 Isaac Sheen, "A Plurality of Gods," *Latter Day Saints' Herald*, vol. 1, no. 12 (December 1860), Cincinnati, Ohio

Snow noted that he was feeling as if he had received some kind of a "sacred communication," but one that he should guard carefully and not teach as doctrine publicly until such a time as he knew, for a surety, that the Prophet Joseph Smith, Junior, himself had taught it. And once he knew that Joseph Smith did, in fact, teach this as doctrine, and not just speculation or theory, then Lorenzo Snow began to testify of it, and frequently at that.[13] At the time that Snow began to publicly declare this doctrine, we have to keep in mind that he was the President of the Quorum of the Twelve Apostles, with his tenure being from 7 April 1889 through 13 September 1898, when he succeeded Wilford W. Woodruff as the Prophet, Seer and Revelator for the entire church until his death on 10 October 1901. Taking this into consideration, we come to understand that this doctrine was no casual one, easily and early arrived at. That being the case, the demarcation of any Mormon boundary on this doctrine of god man and the plurality of gods cannot really be affixed until Snow's declaration of it as recorded in the *Deseret Semi-Weekly News* of 30 October 1894, as this newspaper was designated as an official organ of the Church of Jesus Christ of Latter-day Saints. Therefore, in my opinion, all other statements by lesser authorities of that church could only be considered as speculations, and not canon.

The rivalry between the church at Independence, Missouri, and the one at Salt Lake City, Utah, put the two religious bodies constantly at odds with one another. Sadly, whatever the priesthood of the larger Utah church proclaimed as doctrine or put into action was immediately rejected by the general authorities of the Missouri church.[14] This competitive versus cooperative spirit contributed substantially to the erection of the so-called "Mormon Boundary" in the hierarchy of the reorganization.

Joseph Smith, Jr., the Mormon prophet, 1805-1844. Having provided so much illumination with respect to life on other planets, many are asking, "Was Smith a contactee, or perhaps a 'walk-in' extraterrestrial?" See www.mormonthink.com/glossary/joseph-smith-consent

It should be pointed out that the prophet's son, Joseph Smith, III, while he never outright embraced the *Book of Abraham*, never disparaged it. In an official four-volume history of the church that he co-authored with the church historian, Herman C. Smith, Joseph Smith, III, declared, "The church has never to our knowledge taken any action on this work, either to endorse or condemn; so it cannot be said to be a church publication nor can the church be held to answer for the correctness of its teachings. Joseph Smith, as the translator, is committed of course to the correctness of the translation, but not necessarily to the endorsement of its historical or doctrinal contents."[15]

Howard signals that perhaps this is an easy cop out for the church. If Joseph Smith, Jr., is to be considered as having acted only as a scholarly translator of the Egyptian hieroglyphs comprising the *Book of Abraham*, then any doctrinal teachings of the book that one may find any objection to, cannot be laid at

13 *Biography and Family Record of Lorenzo Snow,*46–47; "Glory Awaiting the Saints,"*Deseret Semi-Weekly News,*Salt Lake City, Utah, 30 October 1894, 1.

14 Howard, *Restoration Scriptures*, 202

15 Herman C. Smith and Joseph Smith, III, *History of the Reorganized Church of Jesus Christ of Latter Day Saints* (Lamoni, Iowa: Herald House, 1896), 2:569.

the feet of Joseph Smith, Jr., as either a religious leader or a latter-day prophet of God.[16]

Advanced Doctrinal Teachings

This is in juxtaposition to the official stance of the Salt Lake City Mormon hierarchy down through history. Of the *Book of Abraham*, the official Latter-day Saints' website (Salt Lake City, Utah), notes that:

> *The Book of Abraham* clarifies several teachings that are obscure in the Bible. Life did not begin at birth, as is commonly believed. Prior to coming to Earth, individuals existed as spirits. In a vision, Abraham saw that one of the spirits was "like unto God" (*Abraham* 3:24). This divine being, Jesus Christ, led other spirits in organizing the Earth out of "materials" or preexisting matter, not *ex nihilo* or out of nothing, as many Christians later came to believe (*Abraham* 3:24; 4:1, 12, 14-16). Abraham further learned that mortal life was crucial to the plan of happiness God would provide for his children: "We will prove them herewith," God stated, "to see if they will do all things whatsoever the Lord their God shall command them," adding a promise to add glory forever upon the faithful (*Abraham* 3:25-26). Nowhere in the Bible is the purpose and potential of Earth life stated so clearly as in the *Book of Abraham*.[17]

New Age Interpretation

Of course, the Christian Gnostics of the first four centuries of the Common Era held similar beliefs. They, like their Greek progenitors, believed in reincarnation, i.e. that our spirits came into being eons before our current birth, and probably have undergone countless incarnations along the way. That Abraham took note of one spirit as "like unto God" is indicative of his identification of the *Angel of the LORD*, or Theophanic Angel, Who is none other than the archangel Michael, also known to us as Jesus Christ, the First Born in the Fullness of Time.[18] And as we now understand, the Gnostic Christians believed that the first Aeon to emerge from the Pleroma was Michael/Jesus Christ. These same Christian Gnostics also maintained that we live our lives in this material world as a sort of schooling, wherein we acquire the knowledge necessary to work good deeds on behalf of our fellow beings and then advance to the next grade in our universal education program. Hence the reference in the *Book of Abraham* for the gods to "prove them herewith," meaning that all must be put to the test and pass it before moving on to some more exalted and higher sphere. This is also in accordance with the teachings of the Swedish scientist and theologian, Emanuel Swedenborg, with respect to the souls on various stages of Venus in its cosmic evolution. Nevertheless, because traditional Christians do not accept these tenets, Mormonism refers to itself as a religion of "restoration." In other words, it brings back, to reestablish the fullness of the Gospel as it was accepted and practiced by the early Christians, to include the Gnostics. The only difference in interpretation of the Gospel between a Gnostic and a Mormon is that while the latter believes in the pre-existence of the soul, he or she does not accept the doctrine of reincarnation. Additionally, while the Mormon does believe that Michael was Jesus Christ in His pre-Earth form, he or she does not accept Him as God incarnate, but only as one of the Eternal Father's many spirit children.[19]

---

16 Howard, *Restoration Scriptures*, 203

17 "Translation and Historicity"

18 Hebrews 12:23 (KJV)

19 Raymond A. Keller, *Venus Rising: A Concise History of the Second Planet* (Terra Alta, West Virginia: Headline Books, 2015), 141.

"Re-symbolization" or Re-imagining in the Community of Christ

That the *Book of Abraham* is no longer utilized in the Community of Christ is symptomatic of an ongoing trend of demythologizing our history and traditions in the church. The period of 1960-1989 was indicative of a theological deconstruction in the Reorganized Church that left the denomination shattered into a "jumble of pieces" where members had to determine, on their own accord, what was important for reestablishing the foundation of their faith. In other words, it became an excruciating chore for members to distinguish what was crucial to Christian belief versus what was incidental. By 1990 and forward to the present day, many members were upset in having the proverbial theological rug pulled out from under them. A goodly portion of these just walked away from the church, with some joining other restoration groups remaining loyal to the testimony and legacy of Joseph Smith, Jr.

This is a scene from Robert A. Heinlein's *Starship Troopers* movie (Touchstone Pictures, 1997), where this Mormon temple at Port Joe Smith came under siege on the Bug Planet.

In the Utah church, for example, Brigham Young is often quoted as saying, "He (Adam) was the person who brought the animals and the seeds from other planets to this world. He brought a wife with him and stayed here."[20] In this case, the Mormon prophet Brigham Young was providing his interpretation of the *Book of Abraham,* Chapter 5. The space age religion preached by Young continues very strong even unto this day. Many elements of traditional Mormonism have even made their way into science fiction. Mormon television program producer Glen A. Larson, the creator of *Battle Star Galactica*,[21] incorporates a Council of the Twelve presided over by Commander Adama. The home of the gods is the planet "Kobol," which is an inversion of the letters that spell out Kolob, the planet of the gods presiding over our galaxy in the *Book of Abraham*. The citizens of the allied planets can marry for "time and eternity." And the uniforms and motifs for the Galactic Federation are decidedly "reformed Egyptian" in character. Additionally, Robert A. Heinlein's *Starship Troopers* sees soldiers dispatched from Earth to defend Mormon colonists on distant worlds where their settlements have been overrun by the indigenous insect inhabitants trying to protect their home turf.[22]

The philosophical theologian W. Paul Jones suggests that the Reorganized Church/Community of Christ, to stem its drift toward Protestant assimilation, might initiate a "re-symbolization of the RLDS[23] tradition."[24] Jones believes that the church has started to undergo this process, having already passed through the periods of restoration and demythologizing. What Jones fears is that the second period, that of demythologizing, went too far. So far did this process go that unless the church as a whole can find an "imaginative application of its tradition's uniqueness," then it will just go the way of other liberal Protestant

20 "Brigham Young versus Joseph Smith, Sen." (sic), *True Latter Day Saints' Herald*, Isaac Sheen, editor, Vol. 1, No. 1, January 1860, Cincinnati, Ohio, page 284.

21 Glen A. Larson, producer, *Battlestar Galactica*, original television series 1978-1979, ABC Network, New York, New York

22 Robert A. Heinlein, *Starship Troopers* (New York City: G. P. Putnam's Sons, 1959).

23 Reorganized Church of Jesus Christ of Latter Day Saints, Independence, Missouri

24 W. Paul Jones, "Theological Re-Symbolization of the RLDS Tradition: The Call to a Stage Beyond Demythologizing," *John Whitmer Historical Association Journal*, Vol. 16, No. 6 (November-December, 1996), 3-14.

denominations, of which there are already too many, some of which are now defunct.[25] When Jones wrote the article in 1996, he prayed for a new prophet to "be imbued with a massive dose of imagination" sufficient to rectify these problems. What he got was President Grant McMurray, who merely accelerated the process of demythologizing by throwing the*Book of Mormon*, Joseph Smith and the restoration legacy under the wheels of the proverbial bus.

I wholeheartedly agree with the objective observer of the church, W. Paul Jones, in his estimation of the situation. For my part, I would like to see, as Jones, the Joseph Smith, Jr., saga re-imagined in the context of the metaphysical and paranormal worlds. I truly believe that Brother Joseph Smith, Jr., was a true visionary and prophet of God who communed with celestial beings on many occasions. I am heartbroken that he is not so recognized in the very church that he established. We all interact with unseen realms on a daily basis, tapping into powers of the Spirit that have hitherto remained latent within us. Brother Joseph gave us the key to reach higher dimensional planes. Let's use it.

And if Brigham Young and Lorenzo Snow were correct in their interpretations of the *Book of Abraham*, then a materialist conception of the universe would follow, much as contemporary astrobiologists posit a process of cosmic evolution. In other words, only with the hypothesis of a special and arbitrary act of creation can we suppose that the Earth is the only planet on which sentient life has come into existence. Other planets have decidedly been proved to have been formed from the same elements and under the same physical conditions as the Earth. Therefore, it logically follows that life is a normal and inevitable consequence of the development of matter; and intelligence must, ergo, be considered as a normal consequence of the existence of life.

To find the gods from outer space we need but take a good look in the mirror.

25 Ibid., 6

Venus Rising

The Kolob Stargate See https://www.lds.org/scriptures/pgp/abr/fac-2?lang=eng. "Fascimile Number 2" in the *Book of Abraham*, included in the Church of Jesus Christ of Latter- Day Saints' scripture volume, the *Pearl of Great Price* (2013 edition), wherein the prophet Joseph Smith gives the following interpretation concerning the insectoid being occupying the center and labeled with the number 1: "*Kolob, signifying the first creation, nearest to the celestial, or the residence of God.* First in government, the last pertaining to the measurement of time. The measurement according to celestial time, which celestial time signifies one day to a cubit. *One day in Kolob is equal to a thousand years according to the measurement of this earth*, which is called by the Egyptians *Jah-oh-eh*." Kolob, as we later learn in the *Book of Abraham*, is the central star system in the amalgamation of stars (*Hah-ko-kau-beam*) to which our Sun belongs (the Milky Way galaxy). The insectoids dwell on Kolob and guard the stargate leading into the presence of God. Incidentally, scientists have discovered a black hole at the center of our galaxy; whence we also learn that power is transferred through tunnels of light energy (*Kli-flos-is-es*) emanating from the revolutions of Kolob to all the inhabited solar systems scattered throughout the galaxy. These are represented by the stars marked 22 and 23 on the facsimile.

In this extract from page 140 of his international awards-winning *Venus Rising: A Concise History of the Second Planet* (Terra Alta, West Virginia: Headline Books, 2015), acclaimed magic realist, mythologist, Theosophist and ufologist, Dr. Raymond Keller, provides a contemporary and unique interpretation of "Fascimile Number 2" in the Mormon prophet Joseph Smith's controversial *Book of Abraham*.

Chapter 2: The Vast Venus Conspiracy

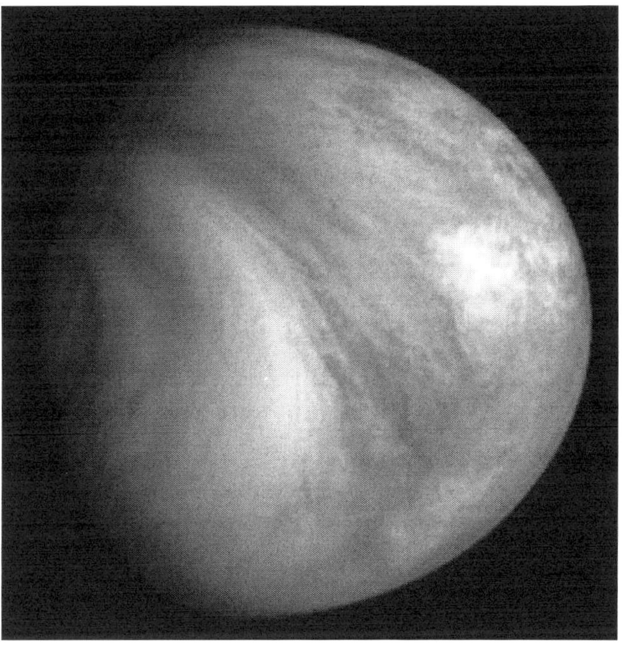

There is a lot that NASA is not telling the public about Venus. Those "in the know" recognize Venus as Earth's sister planet. Both worlds are approximately the same size, have rocky surfaces and water vapor in their respective atmospheres. Fight the "powers-that-be." We want full disclosure now, not only about UFOs in general, but intelligent life on Venus.

"There was a long history of people believing there was life on Venus. It was about the same size as Earth. It had clouds. It was commonly believed it was tropical—wet, hot and steamy."

—David Grinspoon, contemporary astrobiologist

Little did the inhabitants of Earth realize, in the closing quarter of the twentieth century and well into the first quarter of the twenty-first century, that interested eyes from our nearest planetary neighbor were closely observing all phases of our economic, military, scientific and social development, both from aloft in their interplanetary conveyances that we erroneously refer to as unidentified flying objects and on the ground by their agents infiltrating areas where humans were found at play and at work in all walks of life.

With the exception of sensational reports of flying saucers and their occupants in the pages of the tabloid press, hardly a word about these phenomena appeared in the organs of mass market media. And while the National Aeronautics and Space Administration (NASA) was sending probes to the other celestial bodies in our solar system, spokespersons for the agency and other departments of the national government were not telling us the truth about what these robotic ships were discovering about life and the conditions under which it flourishes on the other planets.

Return with me now to the thrilling days of yesteryear, the exciting decade of the 1980s when we were all dazzled by the pulsating rock music of such emerging recording artists as Pat Benatar, David Bowie, Michael Jackson, Cindy Lauper, etc. By 1982, the United States government was still trying to cover up the real findings of its*Mariner 2* that was sent to do a fly-by of Venus twenty years previously. As detailed in my second book in the*Venus Rising* Trilogy,*Final Countdown: Rockets to Venus*(2017), issued reports from the space agency regarding extant but unfavorable conditions for life on Venus were constantly under assault from a growing body of concerned scientists amassing from many technically developed nations.

By February 1982, in an attempt to beat many of these scientific critics to the punch, NASA spokespersons issued press releases declaring that "evidence is mounting that Venus once had an Earth-like ocean." The key word in this dispatch, that was carried by United Press International, is "once;" for the NASA hierarchy wanted the American people to think that while in the distant past life of some kind could have existed on Venus, planetary conditions there had long since deteriorated to the point that nothing in the context of life as we know it could possibly still be there today.

NASA scientists affirmed that "abundant water may have sustained life there long ago." This grudging acknowledgement leads us to believe that we were finally getting closer to the truth of the matter. Throughout the 1960s and 1970s, the intelligence agencies of the United States had accomplished a thorough job in discrediting the claims of the contactees in the eyes of the public, particularly those who attested to contact with Venusian flying saucer pilots, in particular Howard Menger of High Bridge, New Jersey, and the late George Adamski of Vista, California. Both of these gentlemen were the authors of best-selling books on extraterrestrials from Venus coming to Earth in interplanetary spaceships to convey important messages for the future of humankind on this planet.

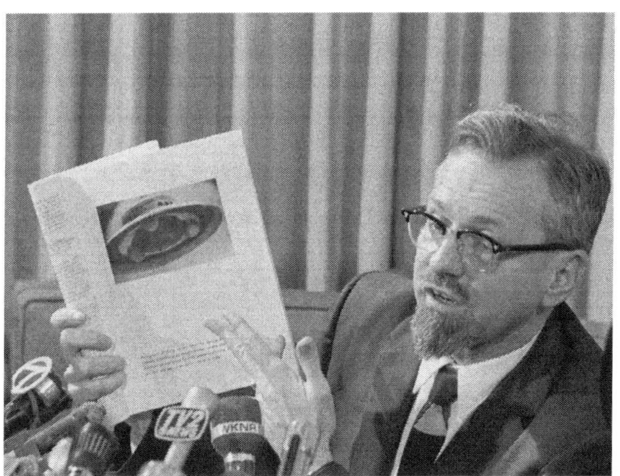

Northwestern University astronomer, Dr. J. Allen Hynek, was contracted with the Air Force Intelligence Center at Dayton, Ohio, and its *Project Bluebook* team to debunk UFO reports in the 1960s. Dr. Hynek is seen here proclaiming that George Adamski faked this photo of a Venusian scout ship, which in his estimation, was fabricated with "parts of a chicken brooder suspended from a fishing line." Later in life, Dr. Hynek would change his tune about UFOs, siding with ufologists like John A. Keel and Dr. Jacques Vallee in maintaining that the objects were real after all and possibly hailing from another dimension in a parallel universe.

NASA's new policy of announcing the possibility of prior life on Venus was proving to be efficacious. Given all of this opposition to the contactees, it is not surprising that only a few in the UFO research community openly questioned it. But some did. A spokesperson for the George Adamski Foundation in Vista, California, informed a local Southern California newspaper that, "Perhaps in time, when officials get ready, the statement 'long ago' will be changed to 'now.'"

This was the first time, however, that scientists began to speak of contemporary Earth-like temperatures existing on Venus, albeit so long ago, maybe even billions of years in the past. Nevertheless, these same researchers were still proclaiming that Venus is an "extreme, dry, cloud-shrouded furnace." At the time of these pronouncements, I remember thinking it odd that no explanations were proffered as to how Venus could possibly support these massive clouds, consisting largely of water vapor, and still be so scorching hot as to merit being called the "hellhole of the solar system."

Venus as Focus of Attention

Venus, alternatively known as the "Morning and the Evening Star," being the third brightest celestial object to grace our skies, and coming in behind only the Sun and the Moon, has often served as the muse for artists, poets, scientists and many other seekers of illumination. Here in the Western Hemisphere, we have come to learn of legends from the indigenous peoples of both Central and South America about gods descending to Earth from the Morning Star. These celestial deities brought the Native Americans in these geographic areas diverse knowledge concerning agriculture, the arts, astronomy, medicine, etc. Venus, being the second planet out from the Sun in its orbital path, is approximately the same size as the Earth, being only some 300 miles less in its diameter. And being the closest planetary neighbor to our world, Venus has naturally become the focus of speculation down through the countless millennia of human history as being an abode of life similar, in many ways, to the biological forms that have evolved here on Earth. This would include humankind.

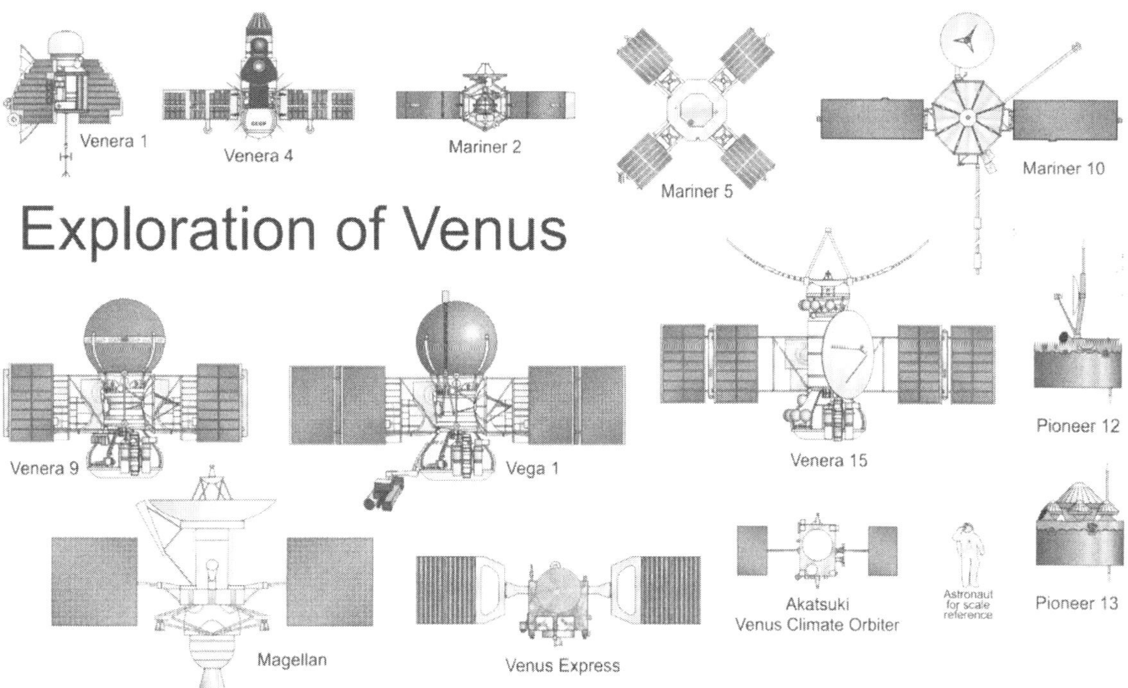

Dr. Raymond Keller, the Venus expert, wonders why the space powers of Earth have sent 43 probes to Venus- that we know of- at a cost in countless billions of dollars. If Venus is the "hell hole" they want us to believe it is, then why weren't most of these spacecraft redirected toward Mars or some other planet? Think about it. See http://www.chartgeek.com/space-probes-chart/.

By the early 1980s, however, the two greatest military powers of Earth, the United States and the Union of Soviet Socialist Republics, had devoted significant resources in fabricating and sending robotic space probes to our sister planet. These spacecraft radioed back signals to monitoring stations in their respective countries of origin reporting that it was just too hot on the surface of Venus for any kind of life, at least as we have come to know it, to exist there. The temperature on Venus allegedly exceeds 800 degrees Fahrenheit. That high of a reading also indicates that lead would literally melt on the surface of Venus. Additionally, the Venus probes from the two superpowers supposedly indicated an atmospheric pressure at nearly 100 times greater than that of Earth. The thick atmosphere itself, according to the data relayed back from the probes, was laden with sulfuric acid.

Many reputable scientists on Earth, from all countries, began to question this data. Based on their own optical astronomical observations, radar, radio spectroscopy, and high altitude balloon instrumentation readings obtained of Venus, they began to suspect that the space agencies of both the Soviet Union and the United States were not being truthful about the information on Venus that they were really garnering from the probe ships. There were just too many discrepancies in the data secured from the probes and the already accumulated base of knowledge concerning Venus assiduously collected over time from Earth-based observation, experimentation and data analysis. Initially, the public at large was disappointed with the probe findings; and this disappointment later turned into a type of complacency. Lethargy with regard to Venus research just set it. But then, as news of scientific objections to the reported findings of the American and Soviet probes emerged, more and more people worldwide began to suspect the existence of a vast and systematic cover-up of the probe data collected directly from the cloud-shrouded planet of Venus. Anything discovered about Venus which would support the existence of life there, even as we know it, was being suppressed on the orders of the powers-that-be. How long could this outrage be permitted to stand?

Soviet postage stamp commemorates the Venus landers.

Soviet *Venera 13* and *14* Probes Land on Venus

On 1 March 1982, the Soviet *Venera 13* soft landed on Venus in a suspected region of volcanic activity. Following this successful landing, on 5 March 1982, another Soviet probe, *Venera 14*, also soft landed on Venus a few hundred miles distant from the *Venera 13* site. However, and this is a big "however," and that being there was a dramatic change in the landing procedures. Both space craft separated from their parachutes at 41 kilometers above the Venusian surface. That would be about 130,000 feet over Venus, whence the probes initiated landing by a process of aerodynamic breaking only. Now it should be noted that both of these *Venera* probes had been substantially reconfigured from previous unmanned vehicles sent to the cloudy planet. This time each of the spherical-shaped probes was capped with a sombrero-like aerodynamic shield. This device served the purpose of slowing down the descent of the probe through the Venusian atmosphere.

Need for the Shield

A prominent writer on space exploration, with access granted to the control room at the Jet Propulsion Laboratory (JPL) in Pasadena, California, commented that, "The dense atmosphere obviously would have made it otherwise impossible to bring these probes down to the ground by parachute. But, in my estimation, here is where the conflict begins." Drawing on his expertise in covering such space matters, the writer noted that, "According to information released from all the earlier US and USSR Venus probes over the past 15 years, all of these probes that succeeded in landing on the planet used the 100% parachute landing technique."

The expert was wishing to remain anonymous. Without a doubt, he would have been denied future access to the JPL control room had he been identified as the one who "spilled the beans" about this discrepancy in landing protocols. But he continued with his explanation, saying that, "This indicates that all of our earlier probes never got there; and the data released was fabricated, unless Venus is, indeed, much like the Earth."

Wow. What a concession. Little by little the truth is outed.

An analysis of the two Soviet spacecraft indicated a spherical shape under a sombrero-like covering. This was a crucial piece of information in understanding the true nature of the*Venera*missions. "But how so?" ....you may be thinking.

Our space specialist surmised that, "The sombrero looks suspiciously like an electromagnetically-propelled device which would not be in need of a parachute descent on any planet. This, in my opinion, would also explain why these probes got to Venus much faster than by solid or liquid fuel rocket propulsion." My own research into these probes indicates that the*Venera 13*was launched on 31 October 1981, with the *Venera 14* going up on 4 November 1981, both going up from the same facility of the Baikonur Cosmodrome in Kazakhstan. The two spacecraft did, indeed, reach the cloudy planet Venus in record time.

Atmospheric Findings Held Back

By June of 1982, the world scientific community was anxiously awaiting information about the content of the Venusian atmosphere garnered from the two probes. This data was in possession of the Soviet Academy of Sciences; but the directorate of the organization was refusing all requests for a release of the findings of the atmospheric studies. They claimed that they had not finished with the project. A spokesman for the scientific body did state, however, that, "The water content in the thick Venus clouds was about 0.1 percent by weight." Unfortunately, he would add nothing more.

There were also some special instruments designed for searching out lightning discharges, of which there seem to be an overabundance on Venus. But there was something odd about this, too. Scientists were dismayed that lightning could be found anywhere on Venus. After all, how could lightning exist in an atmosphere supposedly loaded with clouds of sulfuric acid? I'm not a space scientist, but I do know a little something about electricity. And I think that the strong presence of sulfuric clouds would be considered as self-grounding. The existence of such lightning storms seems so Earth-like. I can imagine all of the scientists outside of the various space agencies just scratching their heads about this. They are probably thinking to themselves, "Can I really believe anything coming out about Venus from the Soviets or the Americans? What are they trying to pull over our eyes?"

Hot Times on Venus

Some of the other equipment installed onboard the probes had been built for the express purpose of detecting volcanism on Venus. Naturally, any such heat-seeking devices would steer the vehicles away from the colder areas of Venus, those parts of the planet covered by mountain lakes or drifting snow, the effect being one of lowering the ambient temperature of these localized landmasses to a significant degree. In the case of the heat-seeking probes, they would have missed these cooler sections of the planet completely, which is exactly what *Venera 13* and *14* did, arriving in an expansive area peppered with volcanoes.

In any event, the Soviet team apparently succeeded in finding active volcanism with their probes, for a spokesperson for the group declared that, "evidence in reference to open volcanic activity on Venus" had been detected by the two *Venera*craft. Just imagine, if you would, a space probe sent to Earth from some alien world being guided over the active Bezymianny volcano on the Kamchatka peninsula in far eastern Russia. This geological feature is located at 56.07N 160.72E with a summit elevation of 2,800 meters above sea level. Any measurements taken of the soil, air and temperature near the top of such an active volcano would certainly parallel any information that was coming back from Venus with the*Venera*probes in a similar region.

I remember when editing the*New Millennial Star*of Hilmar, California, and as I was writing an article about volcanism on Venus, I drew a cartoon for the cover page that had a Venusian scout ship towing an incoming space probe from Earth over the rim of an active volcano and away from a beautiful towering crystal city off in the distance, nestled in the midst of a snow-capped mountain range. Naturally, Venus is no more completely covered by volcanoes than the Earth is. Nevertheless, after this Soviet success in landing two spacecraft on Venus in March 1982, the Houston Space Center released a report to the United Press International announcing that, "Russians find surface of Venus like volcanic soil." To the casual reader, most likely unaware that Venus is a globe nearly as large as the Earth, he or she might erroneously assume that these findings applied to all of Venus. What we see here is just another obfuscation of the facts by NASA, again surely living up to its acronym of**N**ever**A** Straight**A**nswer, at least when it comes to the question of life on Venus, or any other planets.

Dr. Hal Masursky of the United States Geological Survey took note that of the two soil samples gathered by the Soviet Venus probes, the analysis of both rendered similar results. The American scientist was privy to reading the report by Soviet astrobiologist, Dr. V. L. Barsukov, who stated that the surface samples from the*Venera 13*and*14*were "very similar in chemical make-up to basalt, the volcanic rock commonly found on Earth" (See Barsukov, V.L. et al., 1982, "Geochemical studies of Venus surface by *Venera 13* and *Venera 14* spacecrafts," in Russian,*Geokhimia*, 7, 899-919). Dr. Masursky concluded that, "The stew pot on Venus is working in a similar way to Earth's, now that we know the chemistry is the same."

Why is Lady Gaga depicted with a scorpion in her "Venus" single's cover art? You'll find out the amazing answer at the end of this chapter. See also gagadaily.com/forums/topic/188509-why-is-there-a-scorpion-on-the-venus-single-cover-art.

Many Surprises

The photographs of the Venusian surface transmitted back to the Earth by the Soviet Union's *Venera 13* and *Venera 14* landing probes provided many surprises. Planetary geologists were expecting to see a sandy desert under a very dim and distorted light. But what turned up in the photographs was a brightly-lit, orange-tinted landscape with jagged rocks strewn all about. In accordance with the findings of American space probes previously sent to our sister planet, as announced by spokespersons of the National Aeronautics and Space Administration (NASA) in the United States, scientists from around the globe were not anticipating such clear, bright pictures. It was even noted that the distant Venusian horizon was plainly visible in the corner imagery from the *Venera* photographs.

If what the NASA specialists had been telling us all along, that Venus had such an extremely high atmospheric density approaching one hundred times that of the Earth's, then the Venusian atmosphere would have been found to be as dense as water at a depth of 2,000 feet below sea level. What the Soviet photographs revealed was a rock field on Venus, in the vicinity of the *Venera* landed craft, showing only moderate signs of erosion. Many were bound to question the prior NASA explanations as they did not jive with the results coming in from the Soviet Union's dual robotic *Venera* landing craft. NASA analysts of the previous data gathered on Venus by our *Mariner* and *Pioneer* probes had been spouting off about a hot, sand-blown and 800 degrees Fahrenheit Venusian surface, a veritable hell in outer space.

It now became apparent that the Americans' theories about Venus and conditions there needed a drastic revision, and quickly at that, if NASA was going to retain any shred of scientific credibility in academic circles, let alone be believed by the public at large. Returning to Dr. Hal Masursky of the United States Geological Survey, even he thought the *Venera* photographs odd, especially after considering all the disinformation NASA had been previously pumping out to the inquisitive masses about the supposedly much higher atmospheric density and dark, hellish surface conditions. Dr. Masursky, America's leading space geologist at the time, declared that in rummaging through all the *Venera* photographs, "We could not find the great sand dunes we were expecting. We were surprised by the photos of the rocky plain, clean of soil."

And in reference to the posited sulfuric rain that was supposed to be constantly descending from the thick, perpetually dark and overcast Venusian cloud banks, Dr. Masursky opined that, "None has been able to explain where such a self-grounding atmosphere these thousands of Earth-like lightning bolts come from." What was not being stated, however, by Dr. Masursky or anyone else involved with NASA's Venus programs, was that in the previous year representatives of the Soviet Academy of Sciences had approached American scientists contracted with NASA about where, in their estimation, they should steer the *Venera* probes for safe landings on the Venusian surface.

Up to that time, this seemed like a rather strange request, especially when one would compare the Soviet Venus exploration program with NASA's and discover that their achievements in this area, at least, had far surpassed our own. And following the success of the *Venera 13* and *14* missions, a team of Soviet scientists was dispatched to the United States, mostly of Russian ethnicity, to share their landing probes' findings with a consortium of 500 scientists from throughout the Western world. This meeting took place in Houston, Texas, but was closed to the public. So in spite of the economic and political differences that then existed between the two superpowers, it appears as though there was some sort of cooperation between them in the area of concealing information garnered about outer space, but particularly with the planets in

1982 photo from Soviet *Venera 13* probe with clear Venus skies and mountain range in distance. Semi-disc in foreground is the infamous ejected "lens cap." See www.reddit.com/r/space/comments/6z5vlq/image_from_the_surface_of_venus_taken_by_venera.

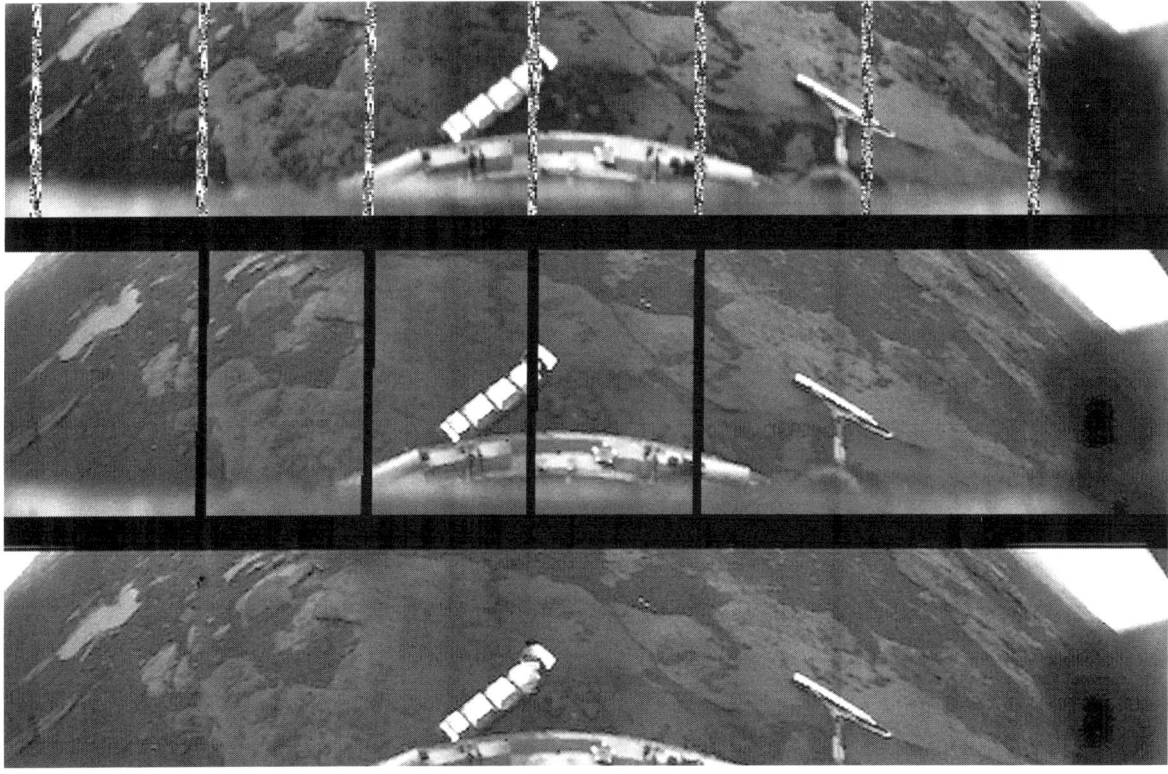

This is a photo taken by the *Venera 10* probe in 1975 of variable Venusian terrain, but shot from a 180 degree perspective. To see a straightened out and reprocessed version by Professor Ted Stryk of Roane State Community College in Oak Ridge, Tennessee, a member of the Planetary Society, please go to danielmarin.naukas.com/2014/07/23/la-superficie-de-venus-como-nunca-la-visto/. Being a land-owner in Datil, New Mexico, I could readily see similarities in land forms on our sister world. There also appears to be a mountain lake in the distance and possible evidence of moss and other types of vegetation.

our solar system and any signs of life above, on or below their surfaces.

The greatest care was taken by both the Soviet Union and the United States when dealing with any data collected that was pertinent to our sister planet Venus. At the secret Venus confab, the conclusion that Venus was once covered with great oceans was allegedly agreed upon by all those assembled. One scientist spoke up, however, and asked the question everyone else in the hall was thinking but was afraid to voice: "Let us suppose," proclaimed the one brave scientist, "that Venus still does have oceans; let's say seventy to eighty percent of its surface is covered by water. This would certainly explain the heavy cloud cover, and the lightning storms."

Spacecraft Deficiencies Noted

At the Houston conference, a glaring deficiency in both of the *Venera* spacecraft was noted. An expert on spectroscopy wondered aloud, "Why didn't the spectrophotometer in both of the *Venera* register the light dust clouds kicked up by the landing of the spacecraft?" The questioning scientist reasoned that since this important instrument failed to detect even the dust clouds churned up from the surface touchdown of the respective *Venera* craft, then what other instrumentation may have also failed to function properly?

Orthographic view of Venus topography as centered over North Pole. Photo comes from files of Jet Propulsion Laboratory in Pasadena, California, as taken by Magellan space probe in 1990. White areas at pole and around equator indicate snow-capped mountain ranges. See www.jpl.nasa.gov/spaceimages/details.php?id=PIA00007.

Orthographic Projections

Back in May 1982, *Astronomy* magazine published a fine arrangement of orthographic projections made of the topographies of the Earth, Mars and Venus. Insofar as the Earth was concerned, the photographs were taken from an orbiting satellite passing over the Western Hemisphere where the Andes, the Rocky Mountains and the poles were clearly seen covered in white. This indicated the presence of snow. Mars, too, was cast in white for its polar regions, in addition to various mountainous terrains. And much to the consternation of NASA scientists, who somehow let the release of these photographs pass by the notice of their censors, Venus was also showing expanses of white, and these were numerous. Those whitened areas of Venus included its immense equatorial mountain range that covers half of the entire sphere from East to West. Other white areas of Venus were also found in its North Polar Region.

Of course, NASA administrators could not let this stand; but it took them a whopping 31 years to come up with a tentative explanation, i.e. that on Venus it actually snows metal. Rose Eveleth, a science writer for the *SMITHSONIAN.COM* website, reported on NASA's unusual "findings" in its 12 June 2013 issue. Eveleth wrote that NASA's Venus experts informed her that, "At the very top of Venus's mountains, beneath the thick clouds, is a layer of snow. But since it's so hot on Venus, snow as we know it can't exist. Instead, the snow capped mountains are capped with two types of metal: galena and bismuthinite."

A NASA spokesperson contended that while the snow on Venus appears to be similar to frost in both its appearance and the way it was created, it really has nothing to do with the water cycle. OK, so it looks like frost and is similarly created; but it isn't composed of water. The spokesperson continued, declaring that, "On the lower Venusian plains, temperatures reach a searing480°C (894°F). This is hot enough that reflective pyrite minerals on the planet's surface are vaporized, entering the atmosphere as a kind of metallic mist, leaving only the dark volcanic rocks like basalt in the Venusian lowlands."

What puzzled me was that the Soviet *Venera* landing probes showed no evidence of this "metallic mist" in any of the photographs taken on Venus. Every *Venera* photograph showed clear, bright skies as far as the camera lens could reach. There was none of this theoretical misting effect actually seen on Venus by the probes sent there of any nation, in real time. In addition, there were no dark volcanic rocks in the lowlands, only in certain areas of the highlands. And neither did the spectrometers detect any of the metals of bismuthinite and galena falling down from the sky in the area or vicinity of any of the higher altitude sites in which the probes had landed. So there's something askew here; and it only gives further credence to the vast Venus conspiracy that has been foisted upon us for the past 60 years or so.

The NASA spokesperson alleges that, "At higher altitudes, this mist condenses, forming shiny, metallic frost on the tops of the mountains. And Earth's simmering sibling has plenty of high altitude terrain. Maxwell Montes, the tallest peak on Venus, stands at an altitude of 11 kilometers (6.8 miles) — 3 kilometers (1.8 miles) higher than Mount Everest."

And NASA seriously wants us to believe that on a mountain 6.8 miles in altitude that searing hot temperatures prevail and that it rains metal from the sky? Talking about science fiction! I, and countless others in the ufology community, have been saying all along that this is pure nonsense. Going beyond NASA and its drab Venus story, let's move on to what the European *Venus Express* probe has discovered about the true temperatures, snow and the polar regions of our sister planet.

Santa Claus Right at Home

The truth of the matter is that Santa Claus himself might find it quite comfortable on the North Pole of Venus, where conditions are quite similar to those found on the North Pole of Earth. At least that is what the results of the European Space Agency's *Venus Express* probe have revealed. Abigail Beal, a science reporter for the United Kingdom's *Daily Mail* newspaper, wrote a series of articles on the real conditions discovered by the European probe in its 22 and 25 April 2016 editions. Some of the conclusions reached by the European scientific team analyzing the data that came in from Venus were that the poles are much colder than anywhere else on Earth and were covered by unusual "atmospheric waves." In addition, the *Venus Express* definitively demonstrated that the atmosphere at the poles of Venus was fàr less dense than anyone had imagined.

Beal wonders why most of the NASA probes sent to Venus supposedly die out after a short duration, while the European probe, much like the Energizer Bunny, continued to transmit important data from Venus. The *Venus Express*was actually the firstVenusexploration mission of theEuropean Space Agency. It was launched in November 2005 and arrived at Venus in

April 2006, whence it began continuously sending back science data from its polar orbit around Venus until 16 December 2015, when the mission was officially ended.

The spacecraft was equipped with seven scientific instruments, with the main objective being the long term observation of theVenusian atmosphere. Such a long period of deployment for a planetary probe had never been done in previous missions to Venus, by any nation or consortium of nations, and proved to be the key to a better understanding of the atmospheric dynamics of our sister world. The results from the Venus probe contributed much to our understanding of atmospheric dynamics in general; and might prove useful in helping climatologists get a better grip on atmospheric and climate changes occurring right hereon Earth. The spacecraft's carrier signal was last detected by the European Space Agency's monitoring station on 18 January 2015. It is believed that at that time the Venus Express had exhausted the last of its propellant. So the *Venus Express,* while originally intended to conduct a mission lasting only 500 days, spent eight years orbiting the cloudy planet before it ran out of fuel.

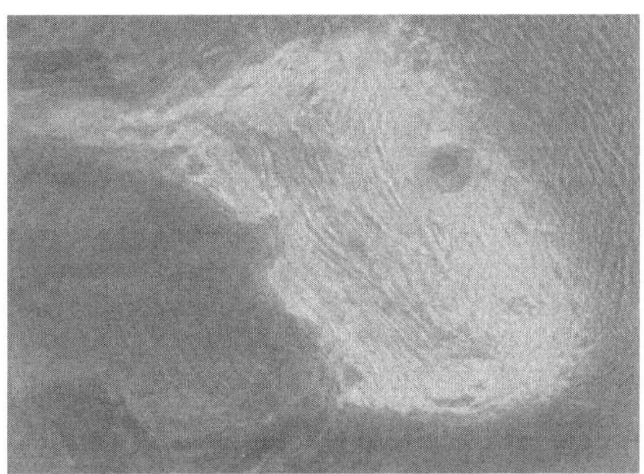

This is the Maxwell Montes region at the North Pole of Venus. Frozen lake clearly seen in the Cleopatra impact crater in the upper east quadrant. See www.unmannedspaceflight.com/lofiversion/index.php/t7276

Authorities at the European Space Agency held a closed-door session in February 2001 to review discrepancies in the findings of NASA's *Pioneer* Venus probe launched in the late 1970s with those garnered by the Soviet *Venera* probes in the early 1980s. The European *Venus Express* was given the green light at that meeting for the purpose of discovering the truth about Venus' atmosphere. They had a sneaking suspicion that the American and the Russian space agencies knew a lot more about Venus than they were letting on. The *Venus Express* would get to the truth of the matter.

Polar Ice Box

The *Venus Express* confirmed that the planet was volcanically active and spun in the opposite direction of most planets. So if you were standing on the surface of Venus, you could watch the Sun rise in the West and set in the East. But most remarkable in the probe's findings was that Venus' atmosphere is rippling with atmospheric waves, both gravitational and planetary, that serve to cool down the Polar Regions to an average temperature of -157°Celcius, or -250.6° Fahrenheit. This would make Venus' North and South Polar Regions, both covered by dual vortex systems that generate these atmospheric waves, colder than any location on the Earth. The vortices apparently serve as a planetary air conditioning system.

The European spacecraft observations also indicated that the Venusian atmosphere, at least in the Polar Regions, was much less dense than anyone else had suspected, by a factor of 40%. Dr. Ingo Müller-Wodarg of Imperial College London, United Kingdom, the director of the Venusian atmospheric study, declared that, "These lower densities could be at least partly due to Venus' polar vortices, which are strong wind systems sitting near the planet's poles. Atmospheric winds may be making the density structure both more complicated and more interesting!"

That the polar region was also found to be dominated by strong atmospheric waves proved to be very important, for this phenomenon is thought to be vital in shaping all planetary atmospheres, including Earth's. Another *Venus Express* project scientist, Dr. Sean Bruinsma of the *Centre National D'Etudes Spatiales* (National Center for Space Studies) in France, also remarked about this phenomenon, "By studying how the atmospheric densities changed and were perturbed over time, we found two different types of wave: Atmospheric gravity waves and planetary waves."

Prophetic Science Fiction

Here's an interesting, but prophetic, excerpt from early science fiction writer, Garrett P. Serviss' novel about the exploration of Venus, *A Columbus of Space* (New York: D. Appleton and Company, 1894):

V*E*N*U*S

Suddenly, with the slightest perceptible bump, we touched the soil, and the car came to rest. We had landed on Venus!

"It's unquestionably, frightfully cold outside," said Edmund, "and we'll now put on these things."

He dragged out of one of his many lockers four suits of thick fur garments, and as many pairs of fur gloves, together with caps and shields for the face, leaving only narrow openings for the eyes. When we had got them on, we looked like so many Eskimo. Finally, Edmund handed each of us a pair of small automatic pistols, telling us to put them where they would be handy in our pockets.

Will an "ice queen" greet future astronauts to Venus? Photo is from advertisement for Disney on Ice's "Worlds of Enchantment." See www.kpbs.org/events/2017/jan/29/disney-on-ice-presents-worlds-of-en/?et=72571.

Our preparations being made, we opened the door. The air that rushed in almost hardened us into icicles!

Lady Gaga gets her "scorpion" on: The photo, on the next page, depicts a scorpion-shaped creature photographed by the rear camera onboard the *Venera 13* Soviet Venus probe in 1982. Dr. Leonid Ksanfomaliti, a premier space scientist in the Russian space program, provided a detailed analysis of the *Venera* photos, taken 30 years previously, to a reporter for a prominent Russian news agency in late January 2012. Of the televised images that came in from the Venus probe, Ksanfomaliti declared, "They all emerge, fluctuate and disappear." A more thorough account of his findings appeared in the acclaimed Russian science magazine, *Solar System Research.*

"What if we forget about the current theories about the non-existence of life on Venus, let's boldly suggest that the objects' morphological features would allow us to say that they are living," added the scientist.

One of the bloggers to the *Gaga Daily* website commented that, "One of the things I love most about Gaga's song 'Venus' is how she intertwines the Greek/Roman mythology with space & planets. So this is perfect, to me!"

Who can disagree? Long live Lady Gaga!

—Cosmic Ray

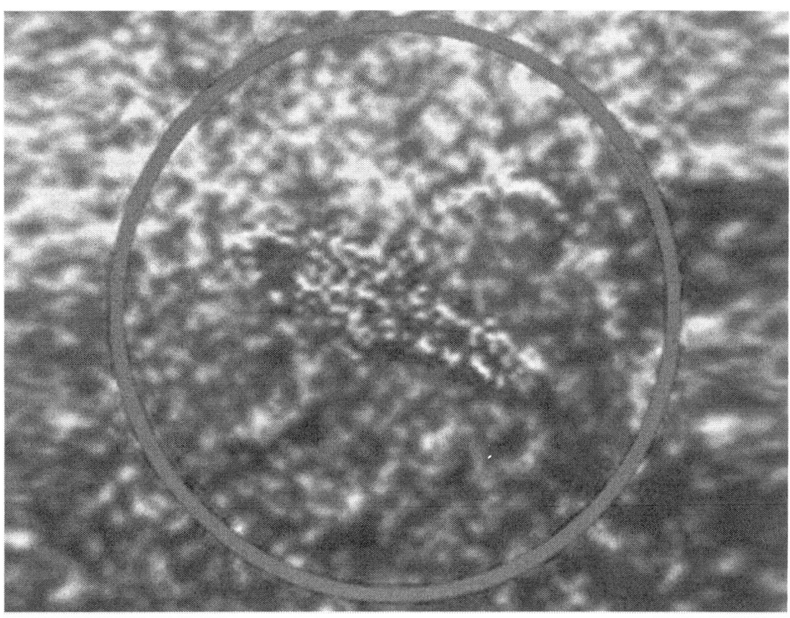

Chapter 3:
The Kenneth Arnold Files

Many thanks are extended to Lon Strickler of Arcane Radio for the above artwork. Lon first ran Dr. Keller's articles on the Kenneth Arnold investigations as a three-part series in his blog, phantomsandmonsters.com.

On 28 March 1950, at the dawn of the atomic and space ages, retired lumberjack Samuel Eaton Thompson of Centralia, Washington, then age 70, came to the rapid realization that we are not alone in the universe and that we can learn much more about extraterrestrials and their way of life simply by remaining calm and exercising our powers of observation. The following is an account of one of the first encounters of an Earthling with beings from the planet Venus in the modern era.

Pre-20th Century Venusian Encounters

The great Persian Sufi mystic, Jalal ad-Din Muhammad Rumi (1207-1273), once declared to his more intimate group of disciples that there were always about 4,000 angels on the Earth at any time. The ministry of angels, according to this learned Islamic theologian, was to help prepare humankind for its ascension into the higher celestial realms, where we, too, might become angels and dwell in the light of eternal splendor. This is our destiny.

In the ensuing centuries since Rumi's preaching, many have pointed to the esteemed presence of angelic beings among us. The most noted Italian poet, Dante Alighieri (1265-1321), hailing from the cosmopolitan city of Florence, in his famous work, the *Divine Comedy* (1320), wrote that the planet Venus was the third sphere of Paradise and that he was accompanied there by his beloved Beatrice Portinari, a young woman that he had been infatuated with since his youth, but who, up to the time he traveled with her to Venus, had only admired from a distance. The two were met at the gates of Paradise by a contingent of angels and other ascended beings that were only too kind to conduct them on a guided tour of the wonders that the enchanted planet Venus had to offer.

Other spiritual insights and revelations pertaining to the realms of angels were advanced by the Swedish mystic, philosopher, scientist and theologian, Emanuel Swedenborg. Obsessed with the concept of an afterlife, he wrote extensively on the subjects of both Heaven and Hell. Swedenborg believed that Heaven and Hell were real, tangible places, but that they were located on other planets in the solar system. Swedenborg claimed that he had actually spoken with beings inhabiting the Moon, Mars, Mercury, Saturn and Venus that had come to visit him here on Earth during various special occasions. He published a book about these close encounters in 1758, *Life on Other Planets*, two centuries before the modern age of the flying saucer contactees. The Swedish scientist believed that the most advanced beings came from Venus. Many of these come to the Earth in the capacity of teachers to illumine our path to a better way of living with each other and preparing our society for its ultimate ascension to a higher kingdom in the celestial realms of light. Swedenborg claimed that after he had become more familiar with some of these exalted beings, they actually flew him across the gulf of outer space to visit the planet Venus, an abode of angels.

Toward the end of the nineteenth century, noted Theosophist, Helena P. Blavatsky (1831-1891), picked up with the heavenly Venus theme where Swedenborg left off. In one of her first metaphysical writings, an essay entitled *History of a Planet* (1887), Blavatsky wrote of the cloud-shrouded sphere that, "Venus is the most occult, powerful and mysterious of all the planets, the one whose influence upon and relation to the Earth is most prominent." From Blavatsky and later leaders in the Theosophical Society, we have come to learn that our sector of the Milky Way galaxy is governed by a council of ascended masters on Venus known as the Lords of the Flame. This august, angelic assembly also includes women. Of course, how could it not? --- at least so far as Venus is the celestial orb that best epitomizes the concept of the divine feminine in so many aspects. Blavatsky gained her specific information about Venus following encounters with ascended masters in the Himalayas.

Besides being credited with starting the "flying saucer craze," Idaho civilian pilot Kenneth Arnold was also one of the first UFO researchers. Dr. Keller gives us a sneak-peak into some of his investigations concerning landed spacecraft and encounters with Venusians.

Flying Saucers: From Venus They Came

The legendary age of flying saucers began on 24 June 1947, when private pilot and fire extinguisher salesman and technician Kenneth Arnold (1915-1984) caught sight of nine disc-shaped objects passing over the tops of the Cascade Mountains in Washington State while flying his Call Air A-2 airplane in the vicinity of Mt. Rainier. Arnold described the movement of these objects as something akin to "saucers skipping across water." On the following day, newspapers from around the globe carried banner headlines about the arrival of "flying saucers" in our skies, and the name has stuck ever since.

Naturally, with his background in aviation and the notoriety that followed his sighting, Arnold was considered the preeminent authority on the subject of flying saucers in our skies well into the early 1960s, when the public turned to prestigious civilian UFO investigative groups like retired Marine Corps Major Donald E. Keyhoe's National Investigations Committee on Aerial Phenomena in Washington, D.C., or Coral and Jim Lorenzen's Aerial Phenomena Research Organization in Tucson, Arizona. Both of these organizations were staffed by highly-acclaimed scientists that served as investigators and consultants in their various specialty areas. The public turned to these groups and others because the United States Air Force was perceived as concealing the truth about flying saucers hailing from other planets.

Arnold took it upon himself to discover the truth that was out there. In the late 1940s through the early 1960s, occasionally accompanied by his wife Doris, he flew throughout the Northwest and investigated hundreds of flying saucer reports. He did this on his own dime and at great personal expense. Arnold also went to great lengths in making sure that he tape recorded all of his investigative interviews with the paranormal experiencers. But the strangest report of all that both Arnold and Doris had the opportunity of investigating came from the Centralia, Washington, retired lumberjack Samuel Eaton Thompson, whose relating of an encounter with some Venusians convinced Arnold that not only did the flying saucers come from our sister planet Venus, but that the Venusians were literally angels operating clandestinely here on Earth.

According to Venus expert Dr. Raymond Keller, many Venusians and other extraterrestrials are attracted to our beautiful beaches. The Venusians, who lack our inhibitions or religious injunctions about nudism, feel no qualms about being in the buff and enjoying nature to its fullest.

Clothing Optional

Thompson's story begins following a visit with family and friends in Markham, located in the western part of the state of Washington. Driving through a forested area along a Pacific coast road, the retired lumberjack noticed a big, luminous, globe-shaped object that appeared to be descending onto the beach, beyond the tree line. Seeing a logging trail that apparently led to the shore, the curious Thompson turned his 1947 black Ford pickup truck onto the dirt road in order to determine just how close he could get to the ocean front. The road narrowed into a small forest clearing, where Thompson conveniently backed up and parked his truck. Hearing a humming noise, like a "swarm of bumblebees," the experienced woodsman pushed his way through the brush and trees toward the beach. In just a few minutes, Thompson had made his way to a rocky shore, whence he ran into "something unheard of." At least that is how he described the initial phase of his encounter to the investigating Arnolds.

Unlike our conventional aircraft that have to come to a landing, this object simply floated a few feet above the ground. But even more surprising was the throng of naked people playing on and beside the steps that led from a door in the bottom of the craft. Of the occupants emerging from the sphere, Thompson took note that they "had the appearance and size of an average teenager, but possessing very fine features." The retired lumberjack also declared that, in his estimation, "They were just beautiful. They had dark tans and lovely, blonde hair that came all the way down to their waists." This uniform appearance of height, skin tone and texture, as well as blonde hair coloring, applied equally to both sexes.

At first, with Thompson merely observing from behind the tree line, he was apparently unseen, or if observed, paid little heed to by the occupants. Thompson, for his part, decided to cautiously approach the ship. At about a distance of fifty feet from the craft, however, he felt an intense flow of heat rushing by him. He told the Arnolds that, "The heat felt like rays from the Sun," and assumed that the radiating effect of its emission contributed to the well-tanned skins of these beings.

As he passed about ten feet beyond the heat barrier and continued to approach the ship, the beings huddled closely together on and about the step ladder, as if they were afraid of him. Thompson, for his part, sensed the fear of the occupants and stated that, "I come in peace and mean you no harm." Apparently, this was considered a satisfactory response by the beings, for they told him that if he removed his shoes and socks, they would let him board the craft, provided that he didn't touch any of the navigation equipment. The beings, in turn, said that they were visitors from the planet we know as Venus, and apologized for their broken English. Except for the ship's captain, they had only heard English and other Earth languages through our radio transmissions.

Once onboard the ship, Thompson would remain the guest of the Venusians for a period of 40 hours. During this time, he discovered that these beings "seemed the happiest and cheerful people I have ever met;" adding that, "Even the smaller ones, their children, were so gentle in their play. They exhibited no roughness or tumbling, stuff like that. They loved to frolic and splash in the water. They were not being told how to behave or think, as is the custom on our world."

For their part, the Venusians were kind and totally benevolent. They explained to Thompson that they would never harm, let alone kill, any human being. The Venusians are here to foster good will among all humankind. But Earth people truly frighten them; for on several occasions, Earthly aircraft have shot down some of their patrol ships. Thompson asked the Venusian captain why she thought that was the case, to which Lady Selene replied that, "The Earth, at its highest vibration level, comes nowhere close to fostering the type of cosmic consciousness that exists on Venus. We, the Venusians, recognize this and understand that humankind is still in the process of spiritually evolving." Interestingly, there have been a few recalcitrant Venusians along the way; but Lady Selene assured Thompson that "These had been banished to Mars for rehabilitation."

Of the many aspects of life on Venus, Thompson discovered that the Venusians incorporate a form of astrology into their religion not unlike that practiced in Tibetan Buddhism. The Venusians, for the most part, are also vegetarians and prefer to eat fruits and vegetables in their raw state. Much like the Seventh-Day Adventists here on Earth, the outstanding dietary habits of the Venusians allow them to live long and healthy lives. Most Venusians live for hundreds of years, as time is measured on our planet, and in a few but special cases, even exceeding thousands of years.

A Tour of the Spaceship

As Thompson asked many of the Venusians technical questions, especially about the ship's propulsion, he was saddened that very few could answer with specific details. When he inquired of this with Lady Selene, the captain explained that her spaceship was an excursion vessel and that the majority of those onboard were tourists. Lady Selene volunteered to take the retired lumberjack on a tour of the ship and to answer his questions to the best of her ability, but also taking in security concerns.

The ship's temperature was set at an equivalent of 80 degrees Fahrenheit. For most Venusians, this is a comfortable setting. And, of course, clothing is optional. The captain asked Thompson if he would prefer to remove his clothing. But being raised in a strict, fundamentalist Christian environment, Thompson politely declined. This prompted the Washington woodsman to ask about such concepts as temptation and sin, to which the captain replied that, "The idea of committing a 'sin' is something that is truly foreign to most Venusians. On Venus, we do not have organized religions like you do on Earth, whose leaders constantly tell you what you must think and do. This is abhorrent to us as critically thinking, and rational, scientific beings. Our way of life is one of charity and kindness to all. Obviously, there are no laws against loving your neighbors as you would yourself, or your own family; and thereby there is no need for regulatory institutions like organized religions. In this regard, Venus is truly an angelic realm."

"I don't understand, Lady Selene. Do you mean to say that there are no churches on Venus?"

"Brother Thompson," said the captain, "a church is not what you think it is- *vis-à-vis* a building of wood or stone. No, a church is merely an assemblage of people. Of course, we Venusians do meet quite often to study and reflect on spiritual concerns. But everyone is a leader in promoting and generating acts of kindness."

"What about Jesus Christ? What do you Venusians think about him?"

"For us, the Venusians, it is not so much about who Jesus is as to what he taught while he lived among you. Jesus approached each individual at their point of need. He blessed them, cured them, taught them, etc. and moved on. He taught his disciples to do the same things and more, changing one life at a time in the process. If you on Earth were to continue in this manner, by the year 10,000 C.E., Jesus will have returned to Earth as an avatar once again, realizing full well that he wouldn't meet the sorry fate he ran into with his last incarnation among the Jews and the Roman occupiers."

The spherical craft was encompassed about by a large, metallic ring. Above the ring were the control and work rooms and below were the living quarters, baths, and recreation centers.

Lady Selene led Thompson into the main control room. "Each ship of this class has four sets of controls," remarked the captain, further adding that, "They consist of little more than levers to make the craft ascend, descend, accelerate or decelerate. Really, these controls are so simple that practically anybody could operate them."

A warning from Venus: Don't lose control of your technology! See futurewarstories.blogspot.com/2014/04/what-will-we-fight-over-robot-apocalypse.

Rage Against the Machines

The captain also provided some wise advice. "Long ago, we made our machines so smart and sophisticated that many Venusians were unable to operate or even understand them anymore. On Venus, we actually went to war with the machines that tried to take over our planet. After a hard-won victory over these 'smart machines,' we returned to a simpler technology that left us in control."

Next, the captain showed Thompson some of living quarters, square rooms onboard the ship, like in an ocean liner, but illuminated without visible light bulbs or fixtures. The walls just seemed to glow with a type of radiant sunlight.

Other rooms shown Thompson included some for bathing and taking showers. Thompson described it thusly: "You just walk into this room and it rains in there, just the same as it rains outdoors. They draw in the moisture from the air; and that is where you'll get your bath."

The adroit woodsman was also escorted into a bedroom. There were beds that folded out from the wall. "Now don't get any ideas," said Captain Selene. "I just thought you might like to check out a bedroom, since you'll be spending the night here." Thompson and the captain chuckled.

Kenneth Arnold, at this point in the interview, asked Thompson about the restroom facilities. Thompson, being the Puritan that he was, said that he never asked about restrooms or used one during the whole time he was on the ship. "So what did you do when you had to go?" asked Arnold.

"When I had to relieve myself, I just went outside, even after dark. Frankly, I have no idea how the Venusians deal with this function because the subject never came up during a conversation. But if it had," Thompson felt that, "the Venusians, who never get embarrassed about anything, would have discussed the subject forthrightly."

Thompson expressed a desire of wanting to go home and fetch a camera, whence he could return and take photographs of the ship and the Venusians, as well as bring some other witnesses back with him. To this the captain emphatically replied, "I'll let you bring a camera back; but it won't do you any good. Also, experience teaches us that not all humans are as nice as you. So bringing anyone else here is out of the question. They might try to destroy us, or even vector some strange disease. We took a chance on you, since our medical monitors showed you were clean after passing through our heat barrier. But I'm responsible for the safety of all these students, so I can't allow them further exposure to other Earth beings."

Thompson did come back in time, right before the ship took off, with his camera. Unfortunately, and true to Lady Selene's words, the pictures he took were no good, just showing huge blobs of light in place of both the Venusians and their ship.

"I'm really impressed, Lady Selene. Do you suppose we of Earth will be able to produce anything like all of this anytime soon?"

"God forbid, Samuel. I don't think the Venusians are ready for Earthlings to move in next door just yet."

Meet the "Venusian Horseman"

Ever since the Boise, Idaho, civilian pilot Kenneth Arnold's radio report of nine disc-shaped objects "moving like saucers skipping across water" above the Cascades, and most notably Mt. Rainier, in Washington State on 24 June 1947, thousands of persons from throughout the world felt confident enough to inform both Kenneth Arnold and his wife Doris of their personal encounters with the mysterious "craft," if that be what they truly are. During the period from the Arnold sighting and the organization of larger and scientific civilian UFO groups in the mid-1950s, most people had no idea who to report sightings of these objects. One might suppose that observers of flying saucers logically assumed that since Arnold had first seen them and had the courage to inform the press of his encounter, then it must be that Arnold could be trusted with the receipt of their report, at least insofar as he would not be judgmental as those who had not seen them would often be. At least Arnold was one individual who had some experience with the flying saucers. Perhaps he might have something to say about an observer's report that would help allay some unfounded fear.

Meet the Venusian Horseman. The "Cosmic Ray" went right to the source to ask the horse. He'll give us the answer that we'll endorse. See www.top5s.co.uk/face-to-face-with-the-man-on-the-black-horse.

"The people have the right to know the facts…."

While Arnold would have liked to investigate all of these reports, he did not have the time or the resources such as would be available to a larger civilian UFO research group to accomplish this task. But let it be known that he did what he could, with him and his wife Doris traveling throughout the American West to interview sundry experiencers with the flying saucers and their occupants. In this chapter, we examine the still little-known case of the visitor from Venus along the Wolverton Trail, taking place in 1955.

The contactee in question was one Oscar F. Knight. He was a very successful rancher living in Central California, just a little to the west of Porterville. He and his wife, Kitty, had owned and managed, since 1950, quite a comfortable ranch where they raised cotton, fruit and walnuts. Speaking for both of the Knights, however, Oscar informed the Arnolds that, "My wife and I are well-liked and responsible citizens. We are only coming out with our story now because the people have the right to know the facts and make their own interpretation."

Knight prefaced his account by stating that, "There is always among our friends someone we particularly enjoy associating with in the great out-of-doors. Such a friendship has been established through the years with Mr. and Mrs. Ken Haladay with I and Kitty." The Arnolds immediately understood that Oscar and Kitty were not going to be the only experiencers in this close encounter.

"OK," said Ken, "just exactly where, and under what circumstances, did your encounter occur?"

"Ken, it was up in the Sierra Nevada in the Sequoia National Park. It's a beautiful place and still contains many virgin areas. One of these special areas is located at Moose Lake, along the Great Western Divide. It's about twelve miles via Wolverton Trail, due east of the park's headquarters."

"What were you doing out there, Oscar?"

"Well, Ken, Kitty and I, along with the Haladays, went up there to go fishing. Not too many people know about this place. It's quite secluded, you know." Oscar went on to explain that they arrived at this site on 1 July 1955, whence they set up camp in the Wolverton Meadow. They felt sure that they were alone up there, with no one closer to them than a few people at the pack station about a mile down a "poor dirt road" meandering through the forest up to their newly established camp grounds.

After devouring some delicious hamburgers that the ladies put on the grill for supper, bedrolls were spread out along the trail, with that being the smoothest place they could find. "We knew that no one went up or down, past us that night," Oscar assuredly proclaimed.

Sleeping undisturbed through the night, the two couples enjoyed a hearty breakfast. The women remained at the camp site, but the men folk adjusted their packs, checked out their fishing equipment, and then made their way beyond a brush area in the mountains. They hiked into a limestone belt where many of the giant redwood trees were located. At about three miles out from their campsite, the men found themselves in a much more rarified atmosphere. Oscar estimated that they were about 8,500 to 9,000 feet above sea level. Naturally, they were tiring quickly as it was a bit more difficult to breath at such a high altitude. They decided to rest for a spell.

Here the trail became wide and clear. Upon looking up ahead for about one-quarter of a mile, the majestic Panther Gap was in view. The panoramic vista was slightly obscured by a few large pine trees. At this point, the gentlemen closely observed the trail, taking note that they were still quite alone.

Kenneth Arnold was deeply moved when Oscar told him that, "Right here an event of destiny was to take place in both Ken's and my life." At this juncture, it should be noted that Kenneth was also the first name of Mr. Haladay, Oscar's fishing companion. And then Oscar continued, "It will forever be branded with clarity into our memories."

"An Event of Destiny"

"What do you mean by 'an event of destiny?'" asked the inquisitive Arnold. "Please go on."

"Well, no one was on the trail. Yet, Ken and I were now startled to see a finely dressed gentleman coming down trail and not over fifty feet above us. He noted from our surprised features that we were mystified at his sudden appearance and made some comment on it.

It was along a trail like this one, in the vicinity of Moose Lake along the Great Western Divide in California that the Knights and Haladays encountered Venusian tourists back in 1955. See plutoniclove.com/2014/06/25/moose-lake-via-alta-meadow-in-sequoia-national-park.

"At once certain things became apparent to us. The stranger was not dressed for this wild woodland setting. From somewhere he had come from a dressing room. Low topped oxfords, brown in color, brown bands of a heavy drill, like whipcord, neatly pressed, light blue shirt; old fashioned wrap-around dress tie. His eyes were different from any I had ever seen. They were a clear transparent brown that one looked into, with depth- not opaque like ours. I was getting a little nervous. I thought this gentleman might be a ghost from the nineteenth century, dressed as he was and appearing out of nowhere."

The intrepid flying saucer investigator was recording everything that Oscar Knight was saying. He then asked Oscar to provide more details about the appearance of this unusual gentleman encountered along the trail.

Oscar continued: "It was easy to place his height at six feet, two inches. I would guess that he was around two hundred pounds, in weight, by our measuring standards. He had a finely featured face that shone with strength and beautiful character. Ken and I would have placed his age in the late twenties, except for a point that would throw our guess off."

"How so?" inquired Arnold.

"Well, as I was saying, he had brown hair. But above his temples there was a fringe of grey. This gave us a feeling that we had no way of knowing this man's real age."

"Go on," said the investigator.

"Additionally, he wore neither coat nor hat. It was certain and obvious that he had not slept in his clothes; nor did he have any pack on his back, nor food and water with him, such as we had."

"That is unusual," quipped Arnold.

"OK, so Ken and I were familiar with this mountainous area, generally. As our new friend sensed this, he started asking us various questions in a manner we had not known of anyone."

"What manner might that be?" asked Arnold.

"His clipped and precise phrasing of words, for one.... I mean, he was cutting each word separately. It was so noticeable. And as the questions came along, a feeling came over me that by thought transference from my mind he had the answers before it was given." Oscar paused for a moment, and then became very animated. He continued, "There was courtesy in his well-modulated voice as he would ask, 'Gentlemen- where- are- you- going?' Gentlemen,- how- high- is- that- peak?' It was as if he had recently learned our language. Following our meeting, we were to go on with our minds searching for answers as to whom our meeting had been with. How little did we know that the mystery was to deepen..."

As the interview progressed, Arnold came to discover that for nearly the rest of that day, Oscar and his fishing buddy Ken were hiking on the north rim of the deep but rugged Buck's Canyon. In the bottom of that canyon flows the middle fork of the Kaweah River; and across from there was the Milk River Ridge, extending for some distance into east and west directions. At the eastern extension, one could see the towering Triple Divide Peak. And in the bottom canyon land could be seen a huge rock. Apparently, in ages past it had broken off from the sidewall of the north rim. The top of that rock is reasonably flat. It was near the Great Western Divide that Oscar and Ken had laid down their packs. Ken suggested that they climb the short distance over a steep barrier in the morning. From this vantage point, the sun could still be seen to be shining. However, down in the great gash below them, shadows were creeping in to warn of the night's approach.

"Blobs of Light" Appear

"Suddenly," Oscar informed Arnold, "I called out in amazement, for five or six moving blobs of light rose up the sides of the large rock, and near these a long string of softly glowing lights. They were so close together that they almost seemed to blend into each other. They appeared as if they were coming from some sort of portholes! The smaller lights came to rest on the big rock surface; while the huge object, which I estimated to be about a quarter of a mile long, began to very slowly rise up to a point about one-third of the way up the shoulder of Milk Ridge Peak. And there it stopped!"

Kenneth Arnold could see that Oscar was highly excited and decided to not interrupt the flow of consciousness emerging from this UFO experiencer. He let Oscar just keep talking.

"Thoughts were racing through our minds," noted Oscar, adding that, "We could hardly give expression to these, so great was our loss for words. We wondered what we were seeing. The strange lights we judged to be about one mile distant.

"Very tired, we rolled into our sleeping bags after some twenty minutes. The lights were still in the canyon." Since the lights had not further approached them nor did the fishermen any harm, they snuggled into their sleeping bags and cut a few zees. With the arrival of the sunrise on 3 July, the two gentlemen were hoping to discover the source of the lights. They looked around but saw no evidence of anything strange in the region below them, where the lights had first become manifest.

The "Horseman" Arrives

Oscar and Ken's excellent adventure was not over yet. They didn't catch many fish on this trip; as all they could think about was the appearance of the oddly dressed gentleman and the phosphorous blobs of light. At this point, one can assume that their hearts and minds were far away from brook trout. Generally, that's how it goes when you are faced with anomalous phenomena like this. Kenneth Arnold understood. Ever since his encounter with the "flying saucers" over Mt. Rainier, he couldn't get them out of his mind either.

Here is the transcript of Arnold's tape recording of Oscar Knight, regarding the subsequent occurrences:

"On our way back, our astonishment could not have been greater, for whom were we to see in almost the same spot, but our genial friend, coming up the trail, this time on a horse! Having been a cowboy for several years, it was plain to me he had not ridden a horse before. The stirrups had not been adjusted to suit the length of his long legs. And this resulted in his knees being placed forward and too high, thus throwing his body out of good balance in the saddle. One hand held the reins very loosely and rested on the pommel."

"Like any good Westerner, I see you are quite the equestrian," said Arnold.

"Thank you, Ken," said Oscar, continuing, "Well, from the smile on his face, it was evident that he was enjoying himself. Stopping the big roan mare in a diagonal position across the trail, he said to us, 'Gentlemen- you- see- I- am- riding- a- horse- today!' I noted the large, full eyes and wide head of the noble horse; and from her looks she seemed to bear a great love shining through her eyes so expressively for everything around her. Here, we got in the only question to ask him, and that was if he had climbed Alta Peak. His quiet answer was, "Yes,- gentlemen,- I- climbed- it- yesterday.'

"Again, we were to reply to several of his questions regarding the scenery and our luck. Knowing he was unfamiliar with horses, I wondered by what means he would start her and was totally unprepared for what he did. Touching with his hand lightly along the poll of the left side of her neck, he spoke with gentle manner, 'Now,- sweetheart,- now,- Girlie,- come- on- let's- go!' And in an understanding way, she headed up the trail. Will wonders never cease? Why hadn't she tried to go back toward the corrals?

"I then asked the stranger his name, to which he replied, 'You- can- call- me- Arthur.' Then before I could ask him where he was from, I received an impression in my mind, as if by thought transference, that he was from the planet we know as Venus, being the second one out from the Sun and the closest one to the Earth.

"When I asked him what he was doing here, he said that he and his friends often visit this canyon as well as other wilderness spots on Earth. Wondering in my mind what was so special about this particular canyon to the Venusians, Arthur explained that, 'The- seclusion- of- this- area- makes- it- an- ideal- place. But,- of- course,- it- is- California,- after- all. We- are- all- enamored- by- your- beautiful state.' I suppose the California Tourist Bureau or Chamber of Commerce might like to know this.

"Now, as we parted company with regret, questions were to come more than ever concerning this being who had left such a profound impression on us. Never did my mind cease to search for the answers over which the dawn of light was to come gradually, as my wife and I become deeply interested and started to read as many books about flying saucers and Venusians as we could get hold of. We especially liked that book by Adamski and Leslie."

Naturally, Arnold and his wife Doris were initially skeptical about Oscar F. Knight's report. They had previously investigated a case of some Venusian nudists landing a globular spacecraft on a rocky beach along the Pacific Ocean in Washington State for the purpose of skinny dipping. That was before George Adamski and Desmond Leslie came out with their bestselling book, *Flying Saucers Have Landed* (British Book Centre, 1953), however. And the experiencer in that case had no desire to write a book about it, go on tour, or otherwise profit from the event. So by 1955, Kenneth and Doris Arnold found themselves embroiled in a ufology universe caught up in the sometimes exorbitant claims of the contactees. They wondered if Oscar wasn't looking to just get on the flying saucer contactee bandwagon. In Oscar's case, they decided that more proof would be required to proceed further in the case. There were just too many out there, especially in California, claiming contact with Venusians. The Arnolds decided that while they weren't going to put Oscar's case into the "circular file," they were certainly going to set it aside on the shelf until such a time as further substantiating evidence should emerge.

It wasn't long before proof emerged, however; for towards the end of 1955, retired Marine Corps Major Donald E. Keyhoe came out with his blockbusting book, *Flying Saucer Conspiracy* (Holt Publishing) that included an account of UFO reports over the same area as Oscar Knight and Ken Haladay's encounter with the Venusian light ships and the mysterious man on horseback. On page 31 of that first edition of Keyhoe's book, we find the following: "....this large craft was sighted by park officials on a different date, as it sped past Morro Rock in Sequoia National Park." Major Keyhoe also found out that the object was seen by several people down in the nearby valley.

Further evidence came to the mailbox of Oscar and Kitty Knight on 10 February 1963. At the conclusion of this article the reader will note a signed letter of testimony from a National Park Service ranger at Sequoia, Carl J. Buehler.

Oscar Knight was a devout Christian and believed that celestial revelations to Earth continue long after the age of the apostles, even unto our day. Arnold asked Oscar why he was going public with his encounter, to which the contactee replied, "Oh! Our dear brothers and sisters of Earth who perchance come to read of this report will hopefully come to realization that we are at the dawning of a new age. For we are all God's children; and I truly believe that we are living in the end times. In these latter days, I believe that the arrival of the Venusians is a fulfillment of Jesus' prophecies. He gives us signs of the times in the sky."

Kenneth Arnold, ever the diligent ufologist, asked Oscar Knight if one day it would be possible to meet some Venusians for himself. "I really want to believe you, Oscar. If only I could speak to a Venusian, face-to-face, then I, too, would be convinced of what you have told me this day."

Oscar Knight suggested to Arnold that he read Matthew 7:7 (KJV), which contains these words of wisdom from the Master Teacher Jesus Christ, "Ask and it shall be given you, seek and ye shall find; knock and it shall be opened unto you."

All I can add to that is "Amen, Brother Oscar!"

Thinking Outside the Box

Tahnee Welch played an ethereal alien in *Cocoon*, the Twentieth Century Fox 1985 hit science fiction adventure. How much did this movie reflect the Venusians and other ETs' affinity for aquatic activities and environments?

Kenneth Arnold Speculates

As a direct result of the peaceful Venusian encounters previously investigated by Kenneth and Doris Arnold, and as reported in this website, these two intrepid UFO and paranormal researchers were coming to some amazing conclusions about the Venusian presence here on Earth. In my 2017 London Book Festival award-winning book, *Final Countdown: Rockets to Venus* (Terra Alta, West Virginia: Headline Books), I devote eight pages to the Arnolds, and continue to dig up yet more startling revelations from their files about their own sightings, their research and the evolution of a cosmic consciousness which surely ensued.

In Timothy Green Beckley's *UFO Review*, Number 14, 1982, published in New York City, Arnold detailed some of his evolving views on UFOs and their crews. Beckley, a.k.a. "Dr. UFO," had dispatched an investigative journalist out to the Arnolds' home in Idaho to get the skinny from Arnold himself about what he had learned as to the nature of the enigmatic flying saucers over the years following his famous encounter with nine disc-shaped objects flying in formation over Mt. Rainier in the Cascades in 1947.

The New York journalist was well received by the Arnolds. Kenneth confided to him that he and Doris had subsequently had other UFO sightings; but he was hesitant to talk about it. He explained that during the two times that he was running for governor of Idaho, the media had a field day in mocking his first and most well known flying saucers experience; and this was the cause of much consternation in his home. "I don't want to go that route again," affirmed Arnold. "I probably lost both times because the voters couldn't take me seriously."

The *UFO Review* writer took note that because of the strange movements of the flying saucers, Kenneth Arnold "has long contended that at least some UFOs are other than interplanetary craft." In the article, "'Angel' Theory Offered by Pilot Who Coined Term 'Flying Saucer,'" the unnamed reporter continues, informing *UFO Review*'s readers that Arnold "has theorized that they (the saucers themselves) may be living life forms and not nuts-and-bolts space ships."

At the time of the interview, the Arnolds were living in Meridian, Idaho. While the civilian pilot's ideas about the nature of the flying saucer phenomenon were changing, he still believed that they were real objects. There was nothing imaginary about them. "It was no optical illusion," Kenneth Arnold insisted.

"So please explain this concept of UFOs as living life forms," requested the reporter.

"Sure," said Arnold, adding that, "What I see taking place is that UFOs are serving as a link between the world of the living and the world of spirits. There might be two worlds connecting the living and the dead. Maybe you continue living when you die. I just can't envision myself on the steps of heaven, before God, and playing a harp with a million other souls."

"Definitely, I agree with you, Mr. Arnold. I think an eternity like that would be boring, and pointless, really," replied the *UFO Review* journalist.

"Maybe it has something to do with that," Arnold continued. He also commented that, "At one time my home was even invaded by UFO beings. They remained invisible; but I and Doris could see the indentations they made while walking across our living room rug. And at another time, I saw a UFO which changed its density; so I concluded that these things could be something alive, rather than machines."

Kenneth Arnold's thoughts on UFOs were surely evolving. His speculations about the flying saucers and the beings who piloted them was beginning to find parallels in the works of the famous French ufologist and computer specialist, Jacques Vallee, in addition to those of the American Fortean researcher John A. Keel, both of whom were advancing a similar view about these type of phenomena being largely associated with inter-dimensional intrusions into our reality, our space-time continuum, as it were.

Venus as an Ethereal Realm

One of my closest friends, counted among America's premier ufologists investigating contactee phenomena, Frank Chille of New Jersey, is himself a UFO experiencer with a particular interest in the activities of Venusians here on Earth. Frank and I were honored guests of Rob Potter's Promise Revealed annual Mt. Shasta conference from 27-29 July 2018, along with the more well-known "Woman from Venus," the one and only Omnec Onec. At a recent UFO meeting in the Trenton, New Jersey, area, Frank and I were conversing about the inter-dimensionality of all the planets in the solar system. Being a life-long Theosophist, I explained that I personally believed that a multiplicity of dimensions permeated time and space, allowing for many more planets within our solar system than we can see with our natural eyes or even detect with most of our primitive scientific instrumentation. Frank concurred, noting that, "Many contactees from Meade Layne of the Borderland Sciences Research Association and Connie Menger in the 1950s, to Omnec Onec and the Master Ching Hai of Taiwan in our times, have all described multiple Venus planets existing in other dimensions. Many contactees have also flown in orbs, scout ships, mother ships or other Venusian vessels; and they have aptly described these as living appendages of the UFOnauts themselves."

Omnec Onec was one of the many experts, along with the "Cosmic Ray" Keller, talking about the advanced civilizations on Venus and what the Venusians have to teach us at the 27-29 July 2018 Mt. Shasta "From Venus With Love" conference. Omnec Onec, the "Ambassador from Venus," brings a message of hope and love to all the inhabitants of the Earth.

Give Peace a Chance

The Venusians arriving here on Earth come in peace for all humankind. They are bringing us celestial knowledge and illumination in order that we may lift up our planet, preparing our brothers and sisters for the work ahead in building a paradise sphere worthy for acceptance into the Galactic Federation of Light. This cosmic organization currently consists of 601 planets in 51 solar systems in an enduring alliance.

All is not work for our brother and sister Venusians. Even while here on Earth, carrying out their important missions, they take time for activities of personal enrichment and recreation.

Photograph of contactee authority, Frank Chille, who shares information on Albert Coe's June 1920 encounter with a Venusian fisherman up in the woods of Ontario, Canada. Frank and the "Cosmic Ray" Dr. Raymond Keller were speakers at the Mt. Shasta "From Venus With Love" conference, 27-29 July 2018, and sponsored by Rob Potter of the Promise Revealed.

They certainly believe in continuing education; and they make time to incorporate such activities conducive to this end into their busy schedules.

Frank Chille learned this about the Venusians from another close friend, associate and contactee, the late H. Albert Coe of Philadelphia, Pennsylvania. Frank noted that the humble Coe was the friend of countless Venusians. His home often served as a safe house for them while they were carrying out clandestine operations here on Earth. Of Coe, Frank tells us that while, "He wasn't special, to be singled out for contact, in any sense of the word; but he was in the right place at the right time to help one of the Venusians who had fallen into a dire predicament…."

To make a long story short, it seems that back in June 1920, Albert and his friend Rod were on a school break. They left their homes in Hastings-On-Hudson, New York, and embarked on a canoeing adventure on the Mattawa River, branching off Lake Trout in the wilds of Ontario, Canada. When the two young men reached a certain spot of rough terrain at a point where the river had significantly narrowed, they decided to separate in order to look for a clear route through to more navigable waters. They were to meet back at the juncture point in a couple of hours and then decide on which route they would take out of the woods. As Albert was making his way through the dense foliage that lay before him, he suddenly heard a man cry out, "Oh, help, help me! Down here!"

As Coe made his way down the gorge in response to the cries of distress, he found a seemingly young man who had apparently fallen into a deep cleft in the rock, getting himself stuck in the process. After freeing him and trending to his wounds, Coe took note of the unusual silvery jumpsuit the man was wearing. He also saw that the man was equipped with an instrument panel strapped across his chest, on the exterior of the suit, and that this apparatus had been smashed in his fall.

Coe inquired as to what the man was doing in such a remote area and was told that he had flown into the area with his "plane," that he had landed in a nearby clearing. He explained that he was looking for a good place to some fishing. That he was flying an airplane in itself would be quite remarkable for the year 1920, when such aircraft were just becoming popular attractions at barnstorming aerial performances. In any event, Coe stayed with the man to help him look for his missing fishing road and tackle box.

The Fly Fishing Venusian

Upon finding the "fishing rod" for the mysterious pilot, Coe noticed that it was highly unusual, exhibiting characteristics that he said were, "the likes of which I had never seen." The rod was bright blue and the fishing line came directly out of the tip. Of course, the pilot was extremely grateful for Coe's kind assistance, both in saving his life and recovering the mysterious fishing rod. The stranger asked Coe for his name and address, for he would "surely write him" at the earliest opportunity.

Coe insisted on helping the man get back to his airplane. As this was 1920, the term "flying saucer" had not yet entered into our vocabulary. But after 24 June 1947 when fire fighting-equipment salesman and private pilot Kenneth Arnold reported nine disc-shaped objects flying in formation at a speed of 1,200 miles per hour, like "saucers skipping across water," Coe would refer to the object he observed with this new appellation. The flying saucer observed by Coe, he would later learn, was a Venusian scout craft. It was quite similar to those sighted by George Adamski and other contactees nearly three decades later.

Before Coe left the area to rendezvous with Rob, albeit late, he learned that his new friend, Zret, was a tourist on Earth from the planet Venus. Zret did write to Coe, as he promised; and they met secretly at many places throughout Coe's life. Coe also encountered many other Venusians and came to discover much about their customs, languages and social mores. Venusians were particularly fond of water sports and activities insofar as they came from largely underground cities situated in played out lava caves in the vicinity of vast aquifers. Most of the surface of Venus was quite arid, except in the mountainous areas where his ancestors, that migrated to Venus from the planet Norca in the Tau Ceti system millions of years ago, had come to settle. They had to leave the world of Norca because of extensive desertification.

MUFON vs. Venusian Nudists

Now it seems that a nudist beach in Wales is catching the eyes of Venusian tourists, according to expert paranormal investigators from the Mutual UFO Network (MUFON) in the United Kingdom. Many visitors to the Morfa Dyffryn beach, situated between the Welsh towns of Harlech and Barmouth, reported a series of strange objects hovering overhead. Among the phenomena are a pure orb-like object and another spherical craft of some sort surrounded by rings. As news of these sightings spread, MUFON investigators began arriving in hoards at the beach, scaring and chasing away the regular nudist crowd, in addition to any Venusians that may have infiltrated their ranks.

MUFON is a designated non-profit research group in the United States. The organization's investigators have taken it upon themselves, however, to mark off the beach as a "place of interest for extraterrestrial activity." The regular nudists at the beach, however, do not appreciate the spotlight that this has placed on their once secluded and comfortable beach. MUFON field investigators have badgered visitors at the Morfa Dyffryn beach to report any sightings even strange sounds to their local chapter, and especially to "take photographs," even if they include Welsh men and women frolicking in the buff. The MUFON notice declares that, "A number of unexplainable sightings have been reported in this area, day and night. Strange lights, plasma balls and other apparitions have been reported. These occurrences have been noted in areas out to sea, the beaches and within the sand dunes." While MUFON says the photographs and other evidence collected will only be "used in the scientific study of these events," the beach goers have their doubts.

Already UFO reports have appeared on MUFON's website, detailing encounters. One incident involved a man and his son walking their dog along the beach. "My son took some photos; and after uploading them to the computer, I noticed this orb-like object on several of them. I put it down to glare from the Sun. However, a few weeks ago a friend posted some pictures on Facebook of an identical orb-like phenomenon, stating they had witnessed the object visually."

Yet another claimed to have sighted a UFO at the beach. "It had five to six glowing rings and was slowly moving in a circle. From the side, it had some lights," noted the observer.

He also added that, "It was standing in mid air for between 5 to 10 seconds. I thought at the moment that it was probably some kind of plane or helicopter. Then it moved really fast and disappeared west and upwards."

A MUFON spokesperson told the reporter Zara Whalen of the *Mirror*, the largest tabloid paper in the British Isles, that, "We are fully committed to the expert and quality analysis of UFOs, as their knowledge is useful to our advancement as a human species. We are a non-profit organization with a focus on enlightening the public about the reality of other intelligent life out there, something the scientific world is growing to realize through their discoveries."

"We live in interesting times."

"We live in interesting times," the MUFON spokesperson continued, "and our knowledge of the planet is advancing every year."

Andy Sayle, the chief executive officer of LIS Aerial Photography, isn't convinced. He first spotted the MUFON sign while flying kites with his children on the beach, just a short distance away from the cordoned-off nudist area. He thought that there might be a more reasonable explanation for the sightings than alien intervention.

"I think the UFOs could be drones operating from a nearby airfield," he opined to the *Mirror*'s reporter. "I would love to believe there really are UFOs, at least until someone comes up with an unequivocal explanation. That said, however, it could quite easily be drones or UAVs (unmanned aerial vehicles) being operated from the nearby airfield at Llanbedr, especially since it reopened a couple of weeks ago."

The MUFON spokesperson was quick to reply. "Well, that would make the members of the Royal Air Force running that airfield guilty as peeping toms."

George Adamski took many excursions to various locales in outer space. Where did you spend your summer vacation? Photo source: www.toptene.com.

Venusian Tourism on Earth – George Adamski Speaks

Despite the alarmist attitude of the MUFON field investigators, there is nothing to fear of the Venusians presence here on Earth. They come in peace and mean us no harm. Because Venus is the closest planet to the Earth, just 26,000,000 miles at its closest approach, our world, with its great biodiversity and oceanic environments, is the prime location for Venusian tourism.

George Adamski, the first "Ambassador to Outer Space," and the author of several UFO books, wrote in *Flying Saucers Farewell* (London, United Kingdom: Abelard-Schuman, 1960), page 74, that, "One studies to learn that he might more fully live according to the will of the Infinite and thereby progress along the pathway to eternal life. Little ones are taught in their homes, as well as in such public institutions. One never grows so old as to stop attending classes of instruction. Periodic travel on their planet and elsewhere through the Cosmos in their gigantic luxury space liners is enjoyed by every individual on Venus, regardless of age. They have learned well that, although one can learn many things through study of records and miniature replicas, travel is a source of unending practical education which gives not only pleasure but lessons of lasting pleasure, never forgotten."

Anyone who remembers a teacher who took care to organize her or his students on a field trip can readily appreciate this sentiment from the great teacher of the mystic arts from the Royal Order of Tibet, George Adamski.

As in the United States, the Mutual UFO Network (MUFON) is actively tracking down extraterrestrial and inter-dimensional visitors from Venus and other spheres of existence. Photo source: London, UK, Daily Mirror, 5 September 2017.

Keller Venus file - K.A. docs

Visalia, California
February 10, 1963

Mr. Oscar & Mrs. Kitty Knight
18331 Road 192
Strathmore, California

Dear Mr. and Mrs. Knight:

From 1951 to 1959 I served the National Park Service as a Ranger at the Ash Mountain entrance to Sequoia National Park and my tour of duty was from 12 PM midnight from May to October, and from 8 AM to 5 PM during the other months of each year.

In addition to my official duties, I was a member of the Ground Observer Corps and all sightings of any type of aircraft were reported immediately to our filter center at Bakersfield, California. This included the reports that came from the numerous fire-watchers on the peaks throughout the 1200 square miles of the parks. I was always in communication by radio to these points as I was in charge of the control station at the park entrance as well as the switchboard which was connected to the entrance station at 9 PM each night.

Each Saturday a total compilation was prepared of all reports from these fire-lookout points together with those sightings from my station on forms provided by the Federal Agency, the United States Air Force, who supervised and for whose benefit the Ground Observer operation was conducted; and it was during this period of service that I did write the report concerning the appearance of a cigar-shaped air vehicle which appeared four days in succession, and maneuvered around Morro Rock; the park superintendent phoned the Fresno National Guard Air Force Unit and jets were scrambled which were air bourn within a matter of minutes, and as if warned by radar, the vehicle took off at fantastic speed and disappeared within a matter of seconds.

Major Donald E. Keyhoe, USMC Ret., at a later date picked up the substance of my report and the same appears in his book titled "The Flying Saucer Conspiracy" on page 31, and this coincides with the date and the place of the experience you have related to me, and was undoubtedly the "Mother Ship" of a number of smaller UFO's, "Flying Saucers" that were sighted many times by hundreds of persons in the park, and I believe these to be of Extra-Terrestrial Origin.

Very sincerely,

Carl J. Buehler

Carl J. Buehler
5035 West Oak Street
Visalia, California

Chapter 4: Venusian Spaceships Are Landing

Follow the adventures of the "Cosmic Ray"/Dr. Keller and the "Queen of Outer Space"/Dolores Barrios in the London Festival of Books award-winning *Cosmic Ray's Excellent Venus Adventure* (Headline Books, 2017).

Strange Experience in Blue Hawaii

In 1946, Sidro L. Basa of 111 Yesler Way, Seattle, Washington, wrote a letter to Raymond A. Palmer, a.k.a. "Rap," the editor of *Amazing Stories* science fact and fiction magazine, in which he detailed a strange encounter he experienced while growing up in Honolulu, Hawaii, back in 1924. Basa, who was in the third grade when the following incident transpired, noted that, "My friend and I decided to play hooky from school and go crabbing at the sand island in Honolulu. I believe that island is around two miles and a half from the shore. It was around 4:30 p.m. when my friend decided to call it a day, and told me if I would want to go home."

Basa continued, "I asked him about his catch and he showed me the crabs that he caught; and he had twice as much as I. So I told him to, 'Go ahead. I'll follow later.' This was because I decided to stay just a little bit longer; and at the same time, I saw a canoe with three little children and a dog approaching. Therefore, I wasn't frightened then, knowing that if there were children, the father or mother should be on the island.

"My friend left me, and as he was far from my sight, the canoe or boat reached the island. They were about 100 yards from me, and they got off the boat and started to run around with the dog. I looked for the mother and father; but so far I did not see either one of them. Surely, I said to myself, they wouldn't be under the water this long. So I was curious, and went to them."

What happened next was like a scene out of Arthur C. Clarke's *2001: A Space Odyssey* (New American Library, 1968). Basa further explained that, "Their two children were still running around, and I approached this one who was sitting down; and as I came closer, he had his face back of me, so I told him, and said, 'Hey, where's your mother?' And as he turned around his head and looked at me, his face was that of an adult, but old and wrinkled."

Basa was startled, to be sure. "I didn't wait for him to answer," he wrote in his letter, adding that, "I turned around and ran as fast as my feet could carry me, and fled for my dear life. I left everything behind me, including my crabs. I could not forget this.... Those little people that I've seen were a little smaller than the midgets in the circus."

Basa lamented that no one seemed to believe him; but editor Palmer wrote back to the witness to this strange encounter that, "We believe you, Brother Basa! And we thank you for reporting the incident to us."

Of course, Raymond Palmer was himself a master of the mystic arts. He was well aware of the ability of ascended entities from Venus to take on the appearance of young people when materializing to human beings on the physical Earth plane. Even Jesus did this, following his resurrection, while speaking with his disciples about the mysteries beyond the world and what would take place in the latter days. In the Gnostic *Gospel of Judas*, the apostle notes that, "Often he (Jesus) did not appear to his disciples as himself, but he was found among them as a child." In the case of the young Sidro L. Basa, having broken the auric field of the Venusian's etheric body by his proximity, he was able to see the master in his true age rather than the reflected projection of the entity's earlier age. See pages 94 and 95 of my *Venus Rising: A Concise History of the Second Planet* (Headline Books, 2016), for further examples of this phenomenon and detailed footnotes.

For the Venusian masters inhabiting Dimension X, everything exists in the "now." See https://kylelatino.deviantart.com/art/2001-A-Space-Odyssey-215999614.

Of course, the arrival of the Venusians on Earth was not well known until the publication of Desmond Leslie and George Adamski's first book, *Flying Saucers Have Landed* (T. Werner Laurie, London, United Kingdom, 1953). That book detailed Adamski's encounter with a Venusian saucer pilot by the name of Orthon near Desert Center, California, on 20 November

1952 in the presence of five witnesses. Photographs and plaster casts of Orthon's footprints were made, so the incident is highly regarded as authentic. Adamski was hesitant to tell of his experience, but felt the public needed to know the truth about flying saucers and life on Venus and other planets. As the first well-known of the contactees, Adamski once described his job as a lecturer and teacher of the cosmic philosophy as being the "hardest job in the world."

Naturally, the world was electrified by Adamski's thrilling account. The flying saucers had been appearing in ever-increasing numbers since the dawn of the atomic and space ages. Adamski explained the burgeoning presence of extraterrestrial spaceships in our skies as being prompted by our advances in atomic weapons and rocketry. That the major military powers on Earth, the United States and the Union of Soviet Socialist Republics, would soon have the ability to launch weapons of mass destruction into outer space was a grave concern to our celestial neighbors. This was especially true for the Venusians, who inhabited the closest planet to the Earth, being just 26,000,000 miles from our world at its closest approach. In cosmic terms, that is just a drop in the bucket.

Early Calls for Disclosure

On 28 January 1956, the Civilian Saucer Intelligence, the world's then largest private UFO investigations group, and the precursor of the National Investigations Committee on Aerial Phenomena (NICAP), conducted a public meeting at Steinway Hall, 113 W. 57th Street in New York City, demanding that the Air Force come clean about the flying saucers. The research director of the Civilian Saucer Intelligence, Ted Bloecher, addressed the issue of increased "saucer landings" with those assembled. The secretary of the organization introduced Bloecher, and noted that while there are no "experts" in the area of flying saucers and their occupants, that "Ted Bloecher perhaps qualifies as well as anyone could, by virtue of his extensive critical study of several hundred reports of this kind."

Bloecher was disappointed that the subject of flying saucer occupants was "generally dismissed by the lay public as a mere joke," adding that, "Even among the better informed there is often a pronounced bias against the idea of 'little men.'

"But a case against the alleged saucer occupants on principle alone will not stand up. For those who have accepted an off-Earth hypothesis as providing the most logical explanation to the reported unique appearance and behavior of the UFOs must assume some intelligence responsible for their recent presence in the Earth's atmosphere. And this presumably means some animate being of one type or another."

The Venusians have been prodding us on for countless millennia. See forums.spacebattles.com/threads/strongest-sci-fi-civilization-the-composite-of-hg-wells-and-jules-vernes-works-can-beat.316142/.

Nothing New Under the Sun, or Over our Heads

The comprehensive Ted Bloecher reported that sightings of flying saucer occupants were "nothing new under the Sun or over our heads." He then proceeded to recount numerous examples of alleged sightings of such entities, harkening back to the great airship flap of 1896 and 1897. During those two years, there was a series of notable reports of unidentified aerial objects. And in several of these reported incidents, the observers described seeing human occupants. Said Bloecher, "The idea of an extraterrestrial source for these 'airships' was largely unimagined in 1896; indeed, numerous people came forth and modestly confessed to knowing the obscure genius who had invented and built the airship, whom they described as looking like an average man, a bearded man but dressed in a dapper uniform. The 'passengers' were also described as looking like ordinary city folk, although a few were wearing what seemed to be some kind of sailor suits." Not surprisingly, it is believed that Jules Verne used these varied accounts of the airship and its occupants as the basis for his fantastic novel, *Maítre du monde/Master of the World* (Pierre-Jules Hetzel, Paris, 1904).

Then there was an account by a gentleman, Joshua Lithbridge of Cardiff, Wales, who provided it to a reporter from the London *Daily Mail* of 20 May 1909. For two months prior to Lithbridge's encounter, Bloecher informed the audience that, "unaccountable objects and lights" had been reported over England, Ireland and Wales; and that on the night of 18 May

1909, while Lithbridge was hiking up in the Caerphilly Mountains, he spotted what seemed to be a "large tube-shaped object sitting on the grass beside the road." Apparently, it had just materialized in mid-air and drifted down softly. There were two people inside, an elderly man and a young woman. Lithbridge informed the reporter that it was a cold night up in those mountains, and that the two occupants inside the tube were dressed accordingly, wearing "heavy fur overcoats." Apparently, the two heard some noise outside and shined some kind of intense lantern on Lithridge. Then they disembarked from the tube, and spoke excitedly to each other in Portuguese or Spanish. Lithbridge could not figure out what they were saying. But then the elderly gentleman told the Welshman that, "Be calm, my friend. We are agents on her majesty's secret service. Please send our regards to Mr. Wells of Sandgate, for he's on the right track!" He patted Lithbridge on his shoulders, and then he and the young woman returned to the tube, whence it just levitated and "sailed away." Lithbridge later took the reporter out to the landing site. All they could find in the light of day was some trampled grass and a "broken fragment of a very small, silver but untitled gramophone record." The reporter turned it in to the newly formed Secret Intelligence Service, what we now know as MI6. Nothing more has been noted of this case; although H. G. Wells, the author of the *Time Machine* (1895), was contacted by the reporter, and the science fiction genius immediately took an interest in the story, peppering the reporter with dozens of questions.

"Cosmic Ray" Keller with two new books in his *Venus Rising* series.

Luke 21:25 (KJV): "And there shall be signs in the sun, and in the moon, and in the stars; and upon the earth distress of nations, with perplexity; the sea and the waves roaring...."

Flying Saucers as a Herald of the Latter Days

The arrival of the flying saucers in our atmosphere at the dawning of the atomic and space ages did not go unnoticed by the ecclesiastical community in the United States. On 5 June 1954, at the conclusion of the General Conference of the Seventh-Day Adventist Church held in San Francisco, California, the entire assembly rose in unison to declare with a loud, missionary voice to the world at large that the strong UFO presence over America signaled the end of an age of greed and selfishness and the fulfillment of the Bible prophecy found in Luke 21:25, that we should look to the heavens for the signs that the time of our global and personal salvation is drawing nigh. Jesus would soon be returning to the Earth, accompanied by his countless legions of angels. Their intention was thought to be that of cleaning up the mess we have created on this beautiful planet that the Infinite Creator has entrusted to our care.

Famed astrologer and psychic Jeane Dixon declared in June 1954 that the flying saucer occupants are "expeditioners from an order of intelligence not known on Earth!" See https://en.wikipedia.org/w/index.php?curid=33720940.

And then just two days later, on the East Coast, the Washington, D.C. *News* ran the following editorial: "….Science just hasn't explained what flying saucers are. We have warned science about this. Two years ago, we told science in no uncertain terms that it had better unwrap this mystery in the larger interest of national sanity. No other country that we know of is so bothered by celestial crockery…. Science, sitting back there with a smug look, isn't doing its job. Now, with another saucer season approaching we say to science…. Put up or shut up."

From psychic quarters, however, doubt was expressed by the great seer, Jeane Dixon, as to any forthcoming disclosures about the true nature of the flying saucers, from either the scientific community or the federal government. Dixon, a long-time resident of Washington, D.C., and the wife of a major car dealer in the area whose batting average in predicting future events was above ninety percent, declared to the National Press Club that, "They (the government officials) are not going to find out what they (the flying saucers) are." But the keen prophetess did remark that she was not to be found in the dark on this critical matter, adding that, "They are expeditioners from an order of intelligence not known on Earth!"

Saucer Intelligences Condemn Racist Attitudes

17 May1954, of course, marked the landmark decision of the Supreme Court case in Brown vs. the Topeka, Kansas, Board of Education, effectively decreeing an end to racial segregation in the nation's public schools. This was the subject getting the biggest "buzz" in Washington, D.C., so to speak, and naturally those in the UFO community were taking a progressive stand on the issue. Keeping in mind that contactee George Adamski would often remark that the Venusians and other extraterrestrials cannot make open contact with more humans until we, as a species, have demonstrated that we can at least get along with our neighbors of different creeds, ethnicities or races, the Venusian commander of the space base Clarion on the far side of our Moon, Aura Rhanes, made an appearance to the editorial office of the Washington, D.C.

Little Listening Post newsletter, to inform the editor, Clara John, and the staff that, "The Venusians have taken note of the increase in familiarity and the casual use of first names in the United States, even for strangers of all backgrounds; and this is very much appreciated." She lamented, however, that so many have had to struggle, and even die, in the cause of attaining equal rights for Black Americans, rights to which Nature and Nature's God entitle them. A reporter from the *Little Listening Post*, a publication that monitors UFO activity on Earth, asked the Venusian commander, "Why do so many have to suffer so in the cause of equal rights? What is the meaning of all this?"

"You have certainly asked a profound question, my sister," said Rhanes. She also added that, "The meaning of suffering is simply that those on this planet have not worked hard enough to better themselves as they have on the Moon base Clarion or other celestial orbs in the solar system, and even beyond. The Earthlings are just too prone to start fights with anyone whom they may not agree. It's hard for the Venusians to even imagine why anyone would fight desegregation. All I can say is just, 'Drat it! Drat it all!'"

THE QUEEN OF SPACE, Mrs. Evelyn Smith of Indianapolis, Ind., buys one of the many books reporting space adventures on sale at the convention.

Mrs. Evelyn Smith attended numerous flying saucer conventions around the United States throughout the 1950s. Here she is seen at the fourth Interplanetary Spacecraft Convention at Landers Field, California, on the weekend of 11-12 May 1957. It was often rumored by many attendees at these events that she was the mysterious Commander Aura Rhanes in disguise.

One of Eric Von Daniken's "Space Gods" takes on a contemporary look. "California Styling" with her 1954 Chevrolet Bel-Air white-topped convertible and sporting a Mickey Mouse Club sweater, Mrs. Evelyn Smith can be seen below, self-identifying as "Aura Rhanes" and posing for Argosy magazine photographer Martin Dain at Second Interplanetary Spaceship Convention held at Landers Field, California, on Saturday, 12 March 1955. Jules B. St. Germain, an attorney and regular writer on paranormal phenomena for Argosy, believed that he once spotted the Clarion commander in the company of contactee Howard Menger out at his High Bridge, New Jersey farm, at a later date.

Always the "shizzle," Clarion Moon base Commander Aura Rhanes momentarily loses her traditional beret and lets her hair down. Photo first appeared in the November 1957 issue of Argosy magazine. To find out more about Aura Rhanes and her mission on Earth, please check out my latest book, *Cosmic Ray's Excellent Venus Adventure* (Headline Books, 2017).

Venus as the Point of Origin

So how can we be so sure that the majority of these extraterrestrials being witnessed throughout the 1950s actually hailed from the second planet of our solar system? Our sister and cloud-shrouded planet Venus as the origination point of the elusive flying saucers was indicated by the observed beings themselves in many ways. One of the more remarkable examples of this was provided by Aasta Solvang and her sister Edit Jacobsen of Mofjell, a village situated in northern Norway. Their report of an extraterrestrial encounter appeared in the 24 August 1954 edition of their local newspaper, the *Nordlands Folkeblad.*

According to Aasta, "We were picking berries when suddenly a dark man with long hair- but otherwise looking very much like an ordinary human being- came out from behind some bushes. He was carrying some kind of valise. We were frightened at first, but the man seemed friendly enough, and stepped toward us."

Then Edit addressed the man in Norwegian, but he didn't seem to understand a word. So then she tried addressing him in English, French and German, but still had no success. It was here where a breakthrough took place. For the stranger then attempted to communicate by "picking up a stick and drawing circles in the dirt around a central circle and what looked like pictures of heavenly bodies along the perimeter of each concentric circle. The third circle out had another small circle outside it and the fourth circle had two additional, smaller circles. Remembering from science class about the solar system, we recognized the smaller circles as being moons."

The two Norwegian women stood by in awe as the artist continued with his drawing. "When he finished this," said Aasta, "he just pointed the stick down onto the second circle. We somehow understood then, through our interpretation of his drawing, that he was showing us he came from Venus. We felt very sympathetic to this man, feeling that he was lost and wondering what we might do to help him out in some fashion."

The Venusian smiled. "Somehow he perceived that we caught his message," said Aasta. She also related that, "The stranger waved for us to follow him, finally leading us to his craft which looked like two flying saucers sandwiched together, about 15 feet across, just a little bigger than a small truck."

Aasta concluded her account, informing the newspaperman that, "The mystery man then opened the hatch, at which time a beautiful tanned woman, looking like a South Pacific islander, and two small children ran out and hugged him. The Venusian then held forth the valise and opened it up, showing the woman, whom I presume was his wife, its precious contents. It was full of berries! The woman said some something in an exotic language that sounded like

Chinese, and the two children jumped up and down, clapping their hands. Everyone was happy and the woman hugged and kissed the man on his lips. All of the Venusians then boarded their craft. The man turned his face toward us, remaining still in the hatchway and waved goodbye with his left hand while bracing himself by holding on to the side of the hatch with his right hand. He closed his eyes for a few seconds and we thought we heard a voice from inside our heads, in our own language, 'Farewell friends and God bless you.'" (Norwegian: *Farvelvenner og Gud velsigne deg.*)

The Venusian followed his family, crawling up inside the flying saucer with the hatch closing slowly behind him. The craft then lifted about ten feet off the ground and began rotating, first slowly, then increasingly faster. "Then," said Aasta, "the entire ship just 'disappeared;' but whether it had taken off at such an incredible speed that our eyes couldn't catch it or it simply dematerialized like a ghost, I could not determine."

Collecting Biological Samples

Apparently, the Venusians are interested in collecting samples of the Earth's rich biodiversity. Perhaps they may have a dual motivation in this. The first motivation may simply be food gathering, as in the case above with the harvesting of berries in Norway. The second motivation may be the collection of diverse plant and other life forms for transport to Venus, where they might be safeguarded and propagated for eventual re-introduction or retransplant on the Earth, following some expected environmental apocalypse in our future. Let's hope that my first suggested motivation is the prevailing one.

Another example of such biological reconnaissance occurred just one month later in Portugal, when three aluminum-suited men climbed out of a flying saucer to do some picking among the flowers and shrubs on a mountaintop near the village of Almaseda, located in the Serra de Guardnha range. The alien beings and their craft were seen by local resident Cesar Cardoso and three other men from the village. Cardoso described all three of the UFO occupants to a reporter from Lisbon's *Diario De Lisboa* newspaper as being over six feet tall. A few days later, the story was picked up by the Auckland, New Zealand *Star* newspaper of 29 September 1954. Cardoso said that the three aluminum-suited extraterrestrials were "cutting flowers, shrubbery and twigs and putting them in a shining box."

Cesar Cardoso and his friends from the Portuguese mountain village politely declined the offer for them to step inside the Venusian scout ship. See https://www.turbosquid.com/3d-models/adamski-venusian-scout-3d-3ds/313047.

Cardoso was the only one in his group of four that dared approach the three alien men. One of them dropped what he was doing in the bushes and came over to talk with Cardoso. The alien asked the Portuguese gentleman, in his own language, "Would you or any of your companions like to enter into our scout ship?"

With that, Cardoso sauntered back over to his friends and asked them, "The visitor wants to know if any of us would like to get aboard the flying saucer." Shaking in their mountain boots, no one was too keen on the idea.

Too close for comfort, Hollywood pulled the plug on a popular science fiction television program. Roy Thinnes as the UFO hunter David Vincent in the opening sequence of ABC Television's "The Invaders," which ran from 1967-1968. Photo source: ABC Television Network, Burbank, California.

Moving again into the presence of the extraterrestrial, Cardoso said, "I'm sorry, Sir, but nobody wants to go in there at this time. They are all just too frightened."

"I can understand that," said the alien, "giving the way your Hollywood productions generally portray the inhabitants of other planets."

Cardoso told the Lisbon reporter that the extraterrestrial did not insist, but kindly assured him at that time that, "We aren't really the monsters you may think us to be. We come to Earth with the purest intentions of love and peace, thinking only of a better future for you and your families. Unfortunately, that future may be some time off."

He and the others then climbed into their scout ship and "flew off vertically at a terrific speed, emitting a shower of sparks" in the process.

Hollywood Muffled about UFO Truth

The Invaders television program, a Quinn Martin production, ran for only two seasons, 1967 and 1968. According to the Rev. Dr. Raymond Broshears of the Long Beach, California, Church of God of Light and contributor, along with contactee Dr. Frank Stranges, to that church's official publication, the *Light of Understanding*, Vol. 2, No. 9, July 1968 edition, the cancellation of the program "was not due to poor viewer ratings," as it had been previously announced by the ABC Television Network. Broshears declared that, "The real reason was due to the impending resignation of Roy Thinnes from the title part. It is said that Thinnes has been threatened on numerous occasions when the show dealt with topics 'too hot to handle.'"

The reverend, like Dr. Frank Stranges, the Earth contact with Venusian space commander Valiant Thor, had an inside track with the moguls of Hollywood. He reached out to the executives at Quinn Martin Productions to put him in touch with actor Roy Thinnes, seeking his take on the situation. "I have no comment other than the fact that there is more truth behind the TV plots than most people realize," is all that Thinnes would say over the telephone before hanging up.

When it comes to UFOs and the truth that is out there, it is safe to say that Hollywood is no stranger to the extraterrestrial connection. From the very beginning of the flying saucer controversy in America, California has led the states in the sheer number of UFOs being observed and reported to news outlets, civilian research groups, law enforcement agencies and military authorities. As recently as 28 December 2017, lifestyle reporter Paula Bolyard of *PJ*

Media reported that California led all the states for the number of UFO reports coming in to the National UFO Reporting Center in Davenport, Washington.

Bolyard wrote that, "California far and away submitted the most reportsof UFO sightings, topping the list with 490 in 2017.Floridawas next with 308, followed byWashington(192), Arizona(180), andNew York(170).New Mexico, home to the famous 1947UFO sighting in Roswell, came in at number 25 with 73 reported sightings. Perhaps surprisingly,Nevada, where the legendary Area 51 is located, reported only 55 sightings, coming in at number 29 overall. North Dakota, Hawaii, and South Dakota had the fewest reports, with 6, 13, and 16 respectively."

Dear friends, keep in mind that the above-cited reports are indicative of aerial phenomena. As to the landing of extraterrestrial, and most notably manned Venusian spaceships in the Golden State, please read on....

From the reels of Hollywood's 1950's retro sci-fi to real-time reports of UFOs, California leads the nation in sparking our imaginations about extraterrestrial life. Pictured above are Venusian bodyguards sent by the Hierarchy of Light to protect a UFO witness that was being harassed by sinister government agents. See https://web2.ph.utexas.edu/~coker2/index.files/sbrothers.shtml.

California as the Epicenter of UFO Research

In 1947, Americans began to witness the appearance of the flying saucers in greater numbers. Many began to wonder about the nature of these aerial phenomena. Were the flying saucers actually spaceships, piloted by beings from another planet? There were rumors circulating of crashed saucers out in the desert areas of New Mexico. These disc-shaped objects were allegedly coming down in the vicinity of nuclear test sites. And on the night of 3-4 September, out at Desolation Valley in California, four campers phoned in a report to the local sheriff's office reporting a "large grey object that passed over with a swishing noise and a rush of warm air." The constable actually came out to the campsite at the break of dawn. What he and the campers saw in the light of day literally blew all of their socks off. There was a circular depression in the ground with an estimated diameter of 50 feet. It was right in the same area where the campers claimed that the object first appeared, seeming to lift itself up and hovering above the desert floor. The details of this saucer landing were first made public in the September 1949 issue of *Fate* magazine.

In the month prior to the publication of the *Fate* article, however, it should be noted that about noon on 19 August 1949, two prospectors in Death Valley, California, reported seeing a "disc crash-land;" but that is not all. They also claim that "two little men jumped out." The dynamic duo gave chase to the seemingly alien beings. Unfortunately, they lost track of them in the sand dunes. When the prospectors returned to their campsite, however, they discovered that the disc-shaped object had disappeared. This encounter was prominently featured in the pages of the 20 August 1949 issue of the *Journal American* newspaper, published on the other side of the United States in New York City.

These two reports straight out of California caught the attention of Ted Bloecher, the Research Director of the Civilian Saucer Intelligence of New York City. Almost nine years later, during his public address in that metropolis' Steinway Hall on 28 January 1956, Bloecher remarked that he was aware of some "very similar cases" coming to light from California. He also felt that it was extremely important that the witnesses not be 'exposed' to publicity in the incidents he was investigating. Notoriety can certainly cloud the view from any possible, objective lens; so Bloecher strived to avoid this type of contamination.

Of some UFO events, Bloecher did feel free to discuss them. It seems that three years back, on 20 March 1953 and once again on 20 May of that same year, two miners had reported a landed disc at the junctions of the Jordan and the Marble Creeks in Butte County, California. One of the miners, John Q. Black, also witnessed the object once more on 20 June. In this latest encounter, Black spotted a little man, perhaps a young boy that emerged from the flying saucer and walked over to the edge of a creek to fill up a pail of water. The extraterrestrial visitor did not seem to be in any hurry after getting out of the craft; but after he caught sight of Black, he scurried back into his ship and sailed away in it, until it passed beyond the horizon. Bloecher notes that this information was garnered from some press dispatches originating from Brush Creek, California, that appeared in the 25 July 1953 of the *World Telegram and Sun* of New York City. This article pointed out that many of the residents of Butte County were expecting the mysterious object to reappear on the twentieth day of July, and were quite disappointed when it failed to show up and thereby meet their expectations. Unfortunately for Black, since the flying saucer did not reappear, Bloecher tells us that, "Black was branded as a hoaxer, though he stoutly stuck to his original story." The Civilian Saucer Intelligence operative, who had later flown out to California to interview Black, was convinced that he was no charlatan or deceiver. "In light of the witness' good character for reliability," Bloecher informed the crowd, all of our Civilian Saucer Intelligence researchers are of the opinion that the story is genuine."

Protecting One's Precious Bodily Fluids

Sometimes the Venusians can get just as thirsty as Florida Senator Marc O. Rubio, taking a big swig of water while delivering the Republican response to President Obama's 2013 State of the Union address.

Spokespersons for the National Aeronautics and Space Administration (NASA) have announced plans to send astronauts to Mars, pending the results of space probes dispatched to that planet and programmed to search for sources of water there. Any manned mission to the Red Planet would not be possible, with our current technology, if there proves to be no water already present on the surface of that distant orb. One of the reasons that so many extraterrestrials are attracted to the Earth is that our planet is an outstanding and seemingly endless source of water, the one substance absolutely required to maintain and keep all of our precious bodily fluids in a harmonious balance.

Venusian Water Run at Giant Rock

The following account of some Venusians siphoning off water from tanks out in the Mojave Desert first appeared in the February-March 1958 issue of the *Proceedings of the College of Universal Wisdom* in Yucca Valley, California. This UFO report was filed by George Van Tassel, the prominent UFO contactee and organizer of the annual Interplanetary Spacecraft Conventions out at the Giant Rock at Landers Field, California, from 1954 through 1977.

Legible scans of the original document are provided at the end of this chapter.

The "Cosmic Ray" Keller operates a projector and explains the history of flying saucers over the city of Paradise, California, to the Paradise Friends of the Public Library on the night of 17 October 2017. More reports of UFOs and close encounters of every kind emerge from Paradise and other cities in Butte County than any other areas of California, including Mt. Shasta. Ufologists Dr. Raymond Keller and Krsanna Duran believe that Paradise and the surrounding area may be the focal point of an inter-dimensional rift connecting the Earth with our sister planet Venus.

Just last year I was up in the city of Paradise, in the same Butte County, presenting my two new *Venus* books in the public library to a capacity crowd. It seems that Butte County has been one of the focal points for intense saucer activity throughout the years; and one of the first flying saucer clubs ever organized in the United States was constituted in Paradise by the pioneer contactees Pal and Dixie Garrett of Kibler Street of that beautiful mountain city. Please check out my third book, *Cosmic Ray's Excellent Venus Adventure*, for a complete rundown on the Garretts' experiences with the flying saucer occupants, as well as their Paradise Interplanetary Space-Craft Club, as well as the meetings, sky watches and pilgrimages of that unique group.

Dr. Raymond Keller speaking in the Paradise, California, Public Library, drew a capacity crowd from throughout Butte County and the state. He reintroduced the city to its glorious past in the history of the flying saucers over California.

Question:
"What time is it?"
Answer:
"Revolution time!"

Radio Free Venus from Giant Rock, California

With Long John Nebel's help, Venusian Commander Aura Rhanes broadcasts her communiqués to the people of Earth live from Giant Rock, California.

Rare photo from Keller Venus files: Always the "Rebel Girl," the Venusian Commander of the Clarion Moonbase Aura Rhanes (center) interviewed by WOR-New York radio personality Long John Nebel (right) on his visit to Giant Rock, California, for the Fourth Interplanetary Spacecraft Convention, on 12 May 1957. Gentleman to the left is contactee Kelvin Rowe, also being interviewed by Nebel. Rowe maintained that beings from the Jupiter and Pluto systems were keeping in touch with him on a regular basis and that all the other inhabitants of the Solar System are standing behind whatever decisions the Venusians want to make regarding the wayward Earthlings and their tampering with vast cosmic powers.

California of Special Interest

Of all locations on planet Earth, the state of California was of special interest to our frequent visitors from Venus. Joe Ramirez, a staff reporter for the Los Angeles *Citizen-News,* wrote an interesting article dealing with this very theme. Appearing in the Friday, 20 July 1956 issue and titled *Valleyites Tell of Venus Men*, the journalist asked if three men from Venus, clad in green suits and riding in "something resembling a giant steel ball," landed in the San Fernando Valley on the previous night. Ramirez noted that three persons in the Van Nuys-Panorama City areas telephoned him Thursday night with this fantastic story. The callers' voices were filled with apprehension.

"But anyway," wrote Ramirez, "all three described the visitors to Earth as tall, about six feet, eight inches, with blond hair which fell about their shoulders, and wearing tight green suits that looked like leotards."

The first of the callers was a Panorama City housewife. She had been out working in her rose garden when the space trio showed up. One of the trio announced to the gardening woman that, "We are from Venus. Be not afraid."

"At first," the woman commented, "I thought this was some kind of stunt from a movie company; so I told them to just get off my property." When Ramirez asked for the female observer's name, however, all he could get was her initials, with these being "M. J."

She explained it thusly: "I'm sorry I can't tell you my real name; but everyone, including my husband, would immediately say that I was crazy."

Then, just minutes after M. J.'s call, the reporter received another one, but this time from a gentleman who identified himself as a 27-year old telephone lineman. He was working up in Van Nuys and also refused to give Ramirez his name. He related some strange occurrence about some "big, strange ball that just dropped about a foot from the pole on which I was working. I was so scared that I felt like getting on top of the pole, but instead, I climbed down and started to inspect the huge ball."

"Just then," the lineman continued, "three guys walked right through the ball and came toward me! The visitors showed no hostility and they even shook my hand. They said they were from Venus and here to help people. They seemed to be holding some kind of mental communication among themselves, but they spoke with their mouths to me.

"These guys said they wanted to help us with their power, and that which the other planets had developed, whereas the Earthlings were still freaks and very primitive."

After finishing his story, he asked the reporter if he could please not call the police. "Why, they will think that I am nuts. And what is more, they'll come and get me, lock me up in an insane asylum, and throw away the key!"

And then Ramirez received his third and still anonymous caller. This was another gentleman from Van Nuys; and this one insisted that he met a "spaceman" last Tuesday morning, around 4 a.m. after he had been awoken by his two barking dogs. He said that, "A huge ball landed in the tree on my front yard, splitting it in half as it settled down. It went right through it, as if the tree were made of butter. I never saw anything like it in my life. Then three men walked right through it and approached me. They told me they were from Venus and that they were friends. The dogs kept barking so loud that these Venusians apparently became frightened, and left. They just got in the ball and vanished.

"Yesterday," the witness continued, "after convincing myself that the whole thing was a dream, I was lying in my back yard when I saw the ball again. This time it was hovering over the house."

What is intriguing about this article is that in all three incidents the witnesses described the Venusians as "looking like humans, generally, except that their eyes did not look real, but appeared to be made of stone." It seems as though all of these reporting individuals had encountered Venusians with orb technology. That they could precipitate the walls of the orb at will is indicative of some type of wave phased oscillation, and perhaps time travel capabilities. Their stone-like, gray eyes reflect the engagement of ultraviolet receptors in their pupils and not necessarily the natural color of their eyes.

Ted Bloecher contacted reporter Ramirez to get clarifying details about the encounters. The journalist punned, "All I can tell you, Mr. Bloecher, is that those Venusians sure have some balls!"

Chapter 5:
The Truth that Was Out There:
Long John Nebel's Fight against the Censorship of Flying Saucer Reports

Silence is the voice of complicity...

See https://occupyoakland.org/2014/03/battle-democratic-pacifica-kpfa/.

"Information is the currency of democracy."

—Thomas Jefferson

Throughout the 1950s and into the early 1960s, the American people came to know the truth that was out there, the truth about the extraterrestrial origin of the flying saucers that traversed our skies on a continual basis. They learned about this great truth from the "contactees," those select individuals privileged enough to encounter and converse with the flying saucer occupants. The platform the contactees enjoyed in broadcasting their message from the extraterrestrials was Long John Nebel's late night radio talk program, *Party Line*, initially transmitted to a geographic listening area covering 25 contiguous states over station WOR in New York City, beginning in 1954.

Born John Zimmerman in 1911, the controversial late night talk show host did not start his career in radio until he was 43 years old. Up until 1954, he held various jobs in sales; and through his running of a successful auction house in New Jersey came into frequent contact with various East Coast radio station advertising sales representatives from whom he purchased air time for advertisements. 1954 was a crucial year for radio. It was receiving a lot of competition from the new and burgeoning television industry. Hence, network radio executives were looking for a new format that would help distinguish their media from television broadcasting. As Nebel proposed a talk show format where listeners could actually call in to the program, and live at that, the radio moguls decided to let Nebel take a hand at implementing his own idea. Nebel's proposal had potential, they reasoned. They had nothing to lose by trying it out, and the world to gain.

Success of the *Party Line*

The program was a great success. It was heartily received by a vast listening audience. After three years on the air, the ufology community could not do without it. Mrs. Clara Walton Colcord John of 4811 Illinois Avenue, N.W., in Washington DC, was the editor and publisher of the famous *Little Listening Post* newsletter, a very important but irregularly published periodical coming out, on average, about every two to three weeks. Mrs. John, however and for the most part, kept her name off of the newsletter. She probably feared government reprisals for her efforts at uncovering the truth about the elusive flying saucers. But she constantly kept her ears open for any breaking news about investigations of saucer reports or related areas of research; and most of all, she was an avid listener of Long John Nebel's *Party Line* broadcasts. In a special bulletin issued by the *Little Listening Post* on 8 February 1957, Mrs. John opined of Long John Nebel that he was "the UFO's best friend in the United States today."

"Long John," she further added, "conducts a unique radio forum from 1:00 a.m. to 5:30 a.m., seven days a week, on Mutual's station WOR in New York. In a few months time a miracle has happened for UFO. Long John's program has metamorphosed from a disc-jockey program into the world's most broad-minded public forum on what Long John calls 'off-beat' subjects: flying saucers, UFO, reincarnation, occultism, extra-sensory perception, psycho-kinesis--- in short: the 'borderland sciences.'"

Mrs. John provides an excellent summary of what the *Party Line* program was for the readers of her *Little Listening Post* newsletter: "Long John calls his program the 'Party Line;' and it is in reality almost that very thing. Guests of the *Party Line* sit in informal groups, munch crackers and drink coffee, around a big table loaded with microphones, in a building full of glowing transmitter tubes, flickering lights, fluctuating meters and big copper coils. They hold completely uninhibited bull-sessions on topics not usually given time on air. Red neon lights flutter and blink on the phones. Long John answers and Party Liners as far away as Canada, Florida and Illinois join in the lively discussions. Within the bounds of propriety, no holds or topics are barred. There are now an estimated 1,500,000 UFO Party Liners, and fan mail often runs to several hundred letters a day. Pillow coddlers are staying awake until dawn, maintaining the 'High Watch' and hearing their pet subjects propounded.... and ufology has come into its own."

While local reports of flying saucers and the opinions of regional flying saucer investigators were plentiful in the great variety of independent newspapers being published throughout the United States and the world at the outset of 1957, radio network administrators were hesitant to go out on a limb in broadcasting such information to the public at large. The charismatic "Long John," so called because of his lanky, thin 6'4" frame, had other opinions on the matter. While he did not necessarily "buy into" every reported UFO or alleged encounter with flying saucer occupants that would pass over his desk, he was more than willing to concede that some of the sightings and incidents may very well be real. Our ignoring of such would accomplish little; and it might even be something that we were thoughtlessly doing at our own peril.

Courtesy of the Gray Barker Collection, Clarksburg, West Virginia: Paranormal and pioneer radio broadcaster Long John Nebel (1911-1978). Nebel interviewed most of the so-called "contactees" of the 1950s and early 1960s on his WOR Radio Party Line call-in talk program. His favorite interview subjects were the ever-beautiful Venusian maidens.

Good Time Slot: Every Ufologist's Dream

Up until the mid-1950s, most radio stations, if they weren't signing off at midnight or an hour or two thereafter, were playing classical music into the wee hours of the morning. With the arrival of the smaller hours of the a.m., most of the turmoil of the city had subsided. The cosmos was lending itself to contemplation by introspective minds. The executives at WOR Radio wisely surmise that such pensive individuals might well be attracted to the kind of thinking person's programming then being proposed by Nebel.

In lieu of this, Mrs. John at the *Little Listening Post* noted that the hours of 1:00 to 5:30 a.m. "are ideally suited to study and investigation and discussion of UFO and all the cosmic subjects which have been crowded off the air by commercials. So---" she added by way of explanation, "Long John converted the psychic hours into a great gift to ufology, contributing much to the great resurgence of UFO interest in the winter of 1956-57. Here, at last, is what every ufologist has dreamed about: frank, public and informative discussion.... for the millions."

With Missionary Zeal

Word of Long John Nebel's intriguing UFO programs had reached the West Coast and wonderful guests like George Adamski of Palomar Gardens and George Van Tassel of the Giant Rock Airport, both situated in California, would make regular stops to the WOR studios when they were on tour in the Eastern states. Visitors from California and other Western states to locations back East situated in the reception area of the *Party Line* broadcast, after hearing a broadcast or two, started to ponder what could be done to provide national coverage for the program. Since the *Little Listening Post* was the most widely distributed newsletter in the American ufology community, editor and publisher Mrs. John made the unilateral decision that everyone on her subscription list, or even anyone with an interest in paranormal phenomena or UFOs should write to the Mutual Broadcasting Company at 1440 Broadway, New York City 18, New York, and "insist that the *Party Line* be put on the Mutual Network, so that all of us can hear it." This was carried out with as true missionary zeal.

Fans of the flying saucers at the time were quick to point out that Mutual Broadcasting Company's radio correspondent Frank Edwards (1908-1967) had been discussing UFOs and interviewing various investigators of the phenomenon since the first appearance of the objects over Mt. Rainier in Washington state on 24 June 1947, as reported by the civilian pilot Kenneth

Mutual Broadcasting Company's correspondent Frank Edwards frequently covered UFO reports on his daytime radio program. Because of the success of Edwards' program, the flying saucer-crazed public demanded, and received, WOR's incorporation of Long John Nebel's program in its late night coverage over the entire North American continent.

Arnold who was flying his Call-Air plane in the vicinity of the Cascade Range on the afternoon of that fateful day. While Edwards was not on the air for four and a half hours every night and aired in the daytime, the subject of flying saucers proved to be both a profitable one for the Mutual Network and a captivating as well as a serious topic for an estimated 10,000,000 listeners. Edwards' program was sponsored by the prestigious American Federation of Labor and had a strong base in the working class.

Mrs. John's advice was followed by the ufology community. They even exceeded the suggestions of the *Little Listening Post's* editor and publisher. Each reader contacted at least three friends in the United States, and even in Canada and Mexico, if they had any dear ones resident in those countries. "OK," said Mrs. John, "continue to urge foreign correspondents to start a *Party Line* in their own countries. It will require thousands of letters to do this. But this is the opportunity that all saucer fans have been awaiting." In ever increasing numbers, people began to listen to Long John Nebel's program to learn about every phase of ufology, in addition to other interesting, but "off-beat" topics. As more were tuning in, they, in turn, would phone their friends and ask them to tune in on the *Party Line*, WOR at 710 on the AM dial, every night from 1:00 to 5:30 a.m., without fail.

"And jam those phone lines," exhorted Mrs. John. "Please phone WOR and participate in Long John's *Party Line*.

"But most important of all," she emphasized, "write to Long John, care of Radio WOR; and tell him you are grateful for the helpful program. Make suggestions and ask questions."

The result was that Long John Nebel's *Party Line* became the first truly North American network program.

High Bridge, New Jersey, contactee Howard Menger (1922-2009), a frequent and most popular guest on Long John Nebel's Party Line radio broadcast, generated a storm of controversy over his claims of meeting Venusians that landed their flying saucer in his backyard apple orchard. Photo is from Keller Venus files.

The sign painter and the Venusians

The subject of flying saucers is what kept listeners' ears glued to Long John Nebel's *Party Line* program, broadcast over WOR-Radio out of New York, seven times a week, from 1 to 5:30 a.m. And of all the experts on this extraordinary subject that ever took a turn in addressing Nebel's ever-growing audience, it was the New Jersey sign painter Howard Menger who proved the most attractive, yet controversial. Ben Gross, a radio and television reviewer for the New York *Daily News*, took note in the 10 February 1957 edition of that newspaper, that the *Party Line* was the perfect venue for the increasing number of "off-beat connoisseurs" in the radio market.

In an article entitled, "Venus Flying Saucer Gave Him a Lift," media correspondent Gross wrote that, "There's a fellow out in High Bridge, New Jersey, who says he has regular contacts with men from Venus. They land in his apple orchard via flying saucers. But that's not all. By means of some mystic mumbo-jumbo, known as teleportation, he vows he can transport his body or any object from one place to another. Air lines, railroads and bus companies, please take notice!"

Gross insisted that he wasn't making this story up and neither had he been imbibing of any alcoholic substances. "No such thing," he insisted; and he added that, "I could pass the drunk test in traffic court anytime.

"The truth is I've been listening these many nights to the *Party Line* conducted by Long John over WOR-Radio; and I've tuned in so assiduously that no matter how fantastic a story you might tell me, I'm eager to listen."

Of course, while the renowned journalist Frank Edwards covered the "nuts and bolts" technical aspects of the UFO phenomenon over Mutual Broadcasting's day-time programming, it was up to Long John Nebel to provide the night owls with all of the esoteric information coming from the contactees, psychics and others tuned into the more metaphysical planes of existence. In this regard, the *Daily News* reporter dubbed Long John Nebel, the "Chef of the Imaginative Bouillabaisse."

Nebel Intrigued

Nebel was particularly intrigued by the contactees and their alleged adventures with extraterrestrials. However, Nebel would be the first to emphatically tell you that he does not necessarily "buy into" all of these contact tales. The pioneer radio talk show personality was definitely a hospitable fellow; and he did manage to keep an open mind about all the paranormal subjects that would come forth on his program, which first aired on 17 August 1956. The guests have proven quite eclectic. Besides the contactees, there have also appeared on the program spiritualists, believers in reincarnation, mental telepaths, practicing astrologers, individuals who can teleport themselves, authorities on cancer and fluoridation, hypnotists, mind readers, escape artists, science fiction writers, magicians, debunkers of bunko schemes, and many more. Often Nebel would bring cynics and doubters on the *Party Line* to hotly engage in arguments with his more flavorful guests as described above.

Over a Steak Dinner at the Pen and Pencil Restaurant

Both being journalists in the Greater New York area, Gross and Nebel agreed to meet over a steak dinner at the famous Pen and Pencil Restaurant, a well-noted hangout for people in the media. Of their meeting, Gross wrote in the *Daily News* that, "John is a 6'4", 170-pounder, with smiling blue eyes and crew-cut brown hair. A former 'mind reader,' carnival and street corner pitchman, band leader, 'super-salesman,' and manager of the world's largest photographic supply store, he glows with boyish enthusiasm."

Gross went on to further describe Nebel. "His youthful zest causes one to doubt the accuracy of his birth certificate, as this formal document says he was born in Chicago, 11 June 1911."

At the restaurant interview, Gross asked Nebel, "Which topic discussed on your show has drawn the most mail?"

"Flying saucers," said Long John Nebel, adding that, "The majority of the 50,000 letters we've received are concerned with these UFOs. Other big mail drawers are teleportation, cancer and fluoridation." Teleportation would be considered the transportation of a material object via mental or spiritual means, through time and space.

Long John Nebel pontificates on flying saucer contactees. Photo is from Keller Venus files by August C. Roberts to Otto Binder for unpublished book.

The Flying Saucer from Venus

The interview continued.

Gross: "What is the story told on your program which you regard as the most interesting?"

Nebel: "That of Howard Menger, a sign painter, of High Bridge, New Jersey."

Gross: "Tell me about it."

Nebel: "Well, Howard is a nice, gentle and average appearing a person as you'd want to meet. He seems to be utterly honest and sincere. He lives in his small home and, according to him, within recent months flying saucers from the planet Venus have landed in his apple orchard three times.

"As he tells the story, which his wife, Rose, says is absolutely true, he has not only talked to outer space visitors who have arrived in a saucer, but actually taken a 17-minute trip with them in their wondrous craft. Furthermore, says Howard, he has 25 witnesses to these incidents. And, of course, he claims he is also regularly in contact with these spacemen via mental telepathy.

"But this isn't the most remarkable part of Menger's many unusual experiences. He says that one night, just a few weeks ago, in response a telepathic message from spacemen, he drove in his station wagon toward Pennsylvania. While driving, he suddenly received another message to turn off a dirt road into a wooded area. He was sitting alone there, but nothing happened.

"Then, apparently with the power he has acquired, Howard teleported himself to his home in High Bridge, some 70 miles away. Or so he claims."

Howard Explained Teleportation

Gross: "How did he do this?"

Nebel: "Howard says he concentrated on appearing at his house. He visualized himself standing before his front door. He saw his sister-in-law answering his knock and Howard took a pipe from his pocket and handed it to her. Then at 8:40, back in the station wagon again, Howard drove to a nearby diner and called his sister-in0-law at High Bridge. She told him that she had just seen him standing in front of the door…. That he had handed her his pipe…. and then had vanished into air.

"And later that night, after Howard had returned home, there it was. His pipe was on a table…. The one he had delivered by teleportation!"

Gross: "What do you think of this story?"

Nebel: "A psychiatrist, Dr. Nodor Fodor, says it's possible, because it's a matter of split personality and involves such things as time, space and another dimension."

Gross: "But, do you believe this?"

Nebel: "Well, you have to admit that it's interesting."

The 'Cosmic Ray' Opines

There is little doubt in my mind that Howard Menger was telling the truth; for I have teleported myself on several occasions. In the introduction to my second book in the Venus trilogy, *Final Countdown: Rockets to Venus*, an account is provided by a witnessing paranormal investigator where I teleported from a youth center in Parkersburg, West Virginia, back to a campsite some ten miles away, in the presence of four witnesses. Attached to this article is a video from my office where I demonstrate how teleportation is accomplished with the aid of a *nimbus*, a Venusian device which augments quantum gravitational compression fields with the aid of an embedded Cytherium/Californium crystal.

Watch Raymond's Video!

https://www.youtube.com/watch?v=4QiEociRIBQ

"Faith is believing in things when common sense tells you not to."

—Fred Gailey in *Miracle on 34th Street* (20th Century Fox, 1947)

The program on the night following Menger's appearance included the channeling of a 50,000 year old spirit from the lost continent of Atlantis. Remember, this was a time when the Congress was considering, at the behest of wayward psychologists, a ban on comic book heroes like Batman, Superman, and Captain Marvel and libraries were routinely being forced to ban books like L. Frank Baum's *The Wizard of Oz* or (1900) or the more contemporary J. D. Salinger's *Catcher in the Rye* (1951). Not surprisingly, a noted Indiana psychologist would launch a campaign to take Long John Nebel's *Party Line* off the air for good, citing it as "rubbish" and declaring that it only served to "cater to those who want to believe in the impossible and the abnormal."

Message of the Contactees

There is a scene in Martin Scorcese's *Last Temptation of Christ* (Universal Pictures, 1988) where Jesus, played by Willem Dafoe, stands before the Roman Procurator in Jerusalem, Pontius Pilate, who is wonderfully portrayed by David Bowie. This is the second time that Jesus appears before Pilate, having been sent back to him by the spineless Herod, who failed to take any action in Jesus' case for fear of any repercussions from either side. Jesus is exhausted from a lack of sleep, and beaten down to a bloody pulp. A group of the Jewish religious leaders have followed the Roman guards escorting Jesus to Pilate's hall. They standby, tucked away in the corner while awaiting the decision of Caesar's representative in Judea.

Jesus between a rock and a hard place: A revolution carried out with love or sword, it's all the same to the powers-that-be. They simply resist any change. Radio broadcaster Long John Nebel and the flying saucer contactees also discovered this same sad fact. The Establishment moved to take Nebel's program, Party Line, off the air, and to have the contactees legally declared to be "insane persons" and to have each one hauled away to the nearest loony bin. See https://giphy.com/explore/the-last-temptation-of-christ.

PILATE
You're back.
(pause)
Hello.
(pause)
So now you're a king. Is that right?

Jesus stares at the sky.

PILATE
Don't look in the air. Look at me. Answer me. I can crucify you. You know that? Now... are you a king?

JESUS
Some say so.

PILATE

Ah yes. Well last time you took that line with me, you fooled me. I don't like to be fooled. What you did in the temple makes it very clear. *You're just another of these religious revolutionaries making difficulties. You take the people into the desert, you talk about God, love, mercy and the new kingdom, but you're just the same as the Zealots.* You all promise glory and bring death. There's a new Messiah every week and a new one dies every week and Rome continues.

JESUS

Remember the statue. And the stone. And the clay feet.

PILATE

How could I forget. Still think your kingdom will replace Rome?

JESUS

No. *My kingdom is not on Earth.*

PILATE

No, it wouldn't be. You're a little smarter than the others. After all, what's a revolution on Earth compared to a revolution in people's hearts?

JESUS

It's a revolution that will come with love, not by the sword.

PILATE

Either way it's dangerous. It's against Rome. It's against the way the world is. And either way, I don't care. Sword or love, it's all the same. I don't care how you want to change things. We don't want them changed. So you know what has to happen. We have a small space for you up on Golgotha. Right next to the bones of your predecessors. Three thousand skulls there, very likely more by now. Maybe you people should go out and count them sometime. Maybe then you'd learn your lesson. But probably not.

***

Now we advance the hands of time to the last decade of the 1950s, where a new set of revolutionaries arrive on the planet. They are also noted for preaching a gospel of peace. Based upon the messages delivered by the contactees on the early broadcasts of Long John Nebel's *Party Line* program, the following information about our brothers and sisters of neighboring planets had been garnered:

1. People, similar in appearance to ourselves, from other worlds in our solar system and beyond, are visiting our planet in great numbers.
2. These space people are in contact with certain political and scientific circles in both the East and West, principally in the Union of Soviet Socialist Republics and the People's Republic of China, as well as in the United States and the nations forming the North Atlantic Treaty Organization.

3. People of Earth, from all walks of life, official and unofficial, have been contacted by brothers and sisters from other planets. Such contacts, however, have been kept secret, at least so far.
4. The philosophy brought to Earth by the contactees can be utilized as an aid in helping us to uncover the truth of our origins and our future destiny among the stars.

Long John Nebel noticed that there was a definite uniformity in the messages being delivered by the contactees over the airwaves on his *Party Line* broadcast. And, as we have noted previously, his Mutual Broadcasting listening audience, and even Nebel himself, were actually starting to act upon these messages, as they are detailed above. Nebel's fans were becoming politically conscious individuals and pressuring the politicians to tell us the truth about the alien presence on our planet and what we can do to prepare our society for its transition into a glorious future in outer space with our brothers and sisters from other nearby planets, even in our own solar system. These planets were most notably Mars and Venus. The contactees on the *Party Line* program were introducing such concepts as free energy, longevity of life into the hundreds of years, freedom from the false religious quackery of the world, and much more. One of the contactees, Dr. Gabriel Green of Los Angeles, California, had even declared his candidacy for president of the United States in the upcoming 1960 election. He would be running on the Flying Saucer Party's ticket. How long could the program continue before the Establishment lowered the curtain on it all?

The successful campaign to get Nebel's *Party Line* broadcast into national syndication provided the effectiveness of the people in organizing from the grass-roots. This was essentially a one-woman endeavor led by Mrs. John, the editor of the Washington, D.C. *Little Listening Post* newsletter that was sent out to a list of active ufologists scattered throughout the United States. Even as I sit here composing this article, I wonder what power each and every one of you, even as a reader, has in restoring this promising message of hope and love to the American people and the world at large. You see, this is exactly what the powers-that-be are fearful of. The presence of friendly extraterrestrials on Earth, lending us their expertise and technology, and once fully known and realized by the masses, will render irrelevant and obsolete all the social structures of command and control implemented by the established order of business, church and state. So thanks to the contactees, if you ever wondered why the last words in the New Testament are "Jesus, come back quickly!" you now have a better perspective.

The Empire Strikes Back: The Opposition Knows No Bounds in Trying to Squash the Truth

As I ponder the efforts of the evil ones to squash the truth that is still out there, my mind races back to this scene from Frank Capra's *Mr. Smith Goes to Washington* (Columbia, 1939). Here the young people rally in support of the beleaguered senator Jeff Smith, who manages to run afoul of the political machine of corruption and graft. While it presumes to rule this country, the people finally start to wake up to the sad reality of the Empire's control matrix and start to think about strategies to take in down, once and for all. See youtube.com/watch?v=EXta_Xr6gl4.

Whether you are coming from the left or the right, you know that this is the case of the situation. This is what the Venusian Clarion Moon Base commander, Captain Aura Rhanes believed; and she said so to her primary contact, the Nevada highways road worker Truman

Bethurum, as well as to Long John Nebel or anyone else who would listen and act upon what she was saying: *that drastic times required revolutionary measures*.

Two Venusian emissaries and revolutionaries sent from Queen Orda of Abejar, Lady Columba (L) and Lady Aurora (R), recently showed up in support of one of Dr. Keller's Venus presentations in a woodlands area in Pennsylvania. Lady Columba was born in Philadelphia, Pennsylvania, in 1902; and Lady Aurora was born in 1880, in Northern India, during the time of the British Raj. Both met in Northern India during the 1930s, and became involved in the struggle of the people of India for independence from Great Britain. Lady Columba returned to the United States before the outbreak of World War II, where she became active with workers' rights organizations in the last years of the Great Depression. Following the war, she moved to Southern California where continued her career as an artist and became a friend and associate of some of the contactees, most notably Truman Bethurum and Buck Nelson. Lady Aurora returned to the mountains above Rishikesh, in Northern India, where she further studied the mystic arts with Ascended Masters and other exalted beings from Venus and other planets.

Opposition to Nebel Intensifies

Once Nebel's program attained national syndication status with the Mutual Broadcasting Corporation, in the summer of 1957, it wasn't long before the opposition mounted. It all began when an Indiana physician and psychologist declared to the Federal Communications Commission that, in his opinion, the *Party Line* talk program should be removed from the air because it was a "strain on mental health."

The 2 August 1957 edition of the New York *Daily News* identifies this complainant as Dr. J. E. Schmidt of Charlestown, Indiana. Schmidt accuses the Mutual Broadcasting Corporation with presenting a program that was essentially "rubbish," and "catering to those who want to believe in the impossible and the abnormal."

The doctor was a guest on John Wingate's *Nightbeat* radio program, where he took the opportunity to denigrate Nebel and the Party Line audience even more. Schmidt said that, "Nebel's audience is composed of 95% neurotics." He also added that, "I will be seeking the help of New York radio and TV writers in my attempt to eliminate this menace from the airwaves."

Some Media Not Co-opted

Ben Gross was the media reporter who wrote this referenced newspaper article, "Should Long John Be Removed from the Air?" While many others in the industry were jumping aboard Dr. Schmidt's anti-Nebel bandwagon, others were still hesitant or outright opposed to the idea of any kind of media censorship. Gross opined that, "The doctor hasn't approached me as yet; but if he does, this is one quarter in which he will find no aid." The reporter explained that Long John's *Party Line* is something that is just too unique in radio, so much so that Gross wrote that, "it was one of the most interesting and novel post-midnight items ever heard in New York and in the other states reached by the program."

While the show was considered somewhat "off-beat" for the times in which it aired, it offered a panel discussion nightly covering a wide range of topics, with such esoteric themes as astrology, haunted houses, hypnotism, flying saucers, numerology, reincarnation, stage and black magic, and even witchcraft, in addition to the more traditional subjects like advertising practices, archaeology, bullfighting, medicine, modern art and music, the stock market fluctuations, and travel.

It was apparent that Gross and others were not going to buy into Schmidt's campaign to knock Nebel's informative program off the air. It was very important for the listeners to keep the *Party Line* on the air, if for no other reason than that it served to bring to the public's attention many topics seldom, if ever, talked about on the airwaves. Reporter Gross summed it up nicely: "*Party Line* is a forum on which hours are devoted to 'kicking around' many little discussed topics. It is the nearest thing to the collegiate bull sessions of recent memory, a veritable Hyde Park of the radio, in that it gives expounders of odd philosophies a chance to be heard."

Perhaps this is what the Establishment mostly fears, some "odd" idea or philosophy catching on with the masses. This would particularly be so in the case where such a concept would prove to run counter to the ruling elite's image of what society should look like or even how it should be managed.

Besides the wide variety of topics the listener encounters on the program, there is always to be found a bevy of experts to discuss them and even answer audience questions that are called in. Naturally, there were no laws, as yet enacted, prohibiting anyone from tuning in to the program. After midnight, in the latter half of the 1950s, one could hear various disc jockeys airing music, from the new fangled rock and roll to symphonies. And then there were other news programs, like Barry Gray's business interviews or Big Joe's charity endeavors. But Long John Nebel offered the real alternative for that "something different" in the morning hours. Gross lamented, therefore, that "To deprive the public of this program would be a flagrant abuse of censorship."

Contactee George Adamski explains power sources and maneuvering capabilities of scout ships and motherships to WOR-Radio New York pioneer talk show host, Long John Nebel. Photo is from archives of Mutual Broadcasting Corporation.

And as to Dr. Schmidt's contention that an "off-beat" radio program could, in and of itself, affect the mental health of a listener, wouldn't it be logical to assume that any adult who would be adversely affected by such program is just already "too far gone," so to speak; and that he or she might really require the services of a psychiatrist well before listening to any kind of broadcast.

Assessment of the Situation

As contactees of the New Age are emerging, there is much we can glean from Long Nebel and the guests of his program like George Adamski, Truman Bethurum, Daniel Fry, Howard Menger and others in the field of ufology that have come and gone before us. All of these cited contactees and many others who graced the *Party Line* show, merely desired that Nebel's audience have the opportunity of knowing what was going on in every aspect of extraterrestrial and UFO research. Hopefully, we of the present age will discover the truth about the contactee messages and turn to face the times to come with a greater bearing and confidence.

Freedom of speech and expression is essential to guarding and maintaining a democratic society. This applies equally to ufology as well as any other topic. While Nebel did not personally believe all of the contactee reports that were disseminated over the airwaves via his *Party Line* program, it is significant that he did not use his platform to either belittle or fight anyone, and all of this in spite of all the pressure on him to do so by Mutual executives and others of the elite beyond the halls of the broadcasting network. Nebel realized that no matter what the truth that was out there was, it would eventually be revealed in the full light of day for the whole world to see and stand in awe at. But in the meantime, it was up to each and every individual to decide what he or she could or could not accept in the contactee claims. Taking this to heart, these individuals could then march on to new and exciting experiences in the fantastic UFO universe and the wondrous worlds of tomorrow which they surely will encounter. So let the economic, military, political and religious powers of the Earth quake in their boots, for their time is numbered and the final countdown has begun.

Chapter 6: Dominick Lucchesi Meets the "Space Girl"

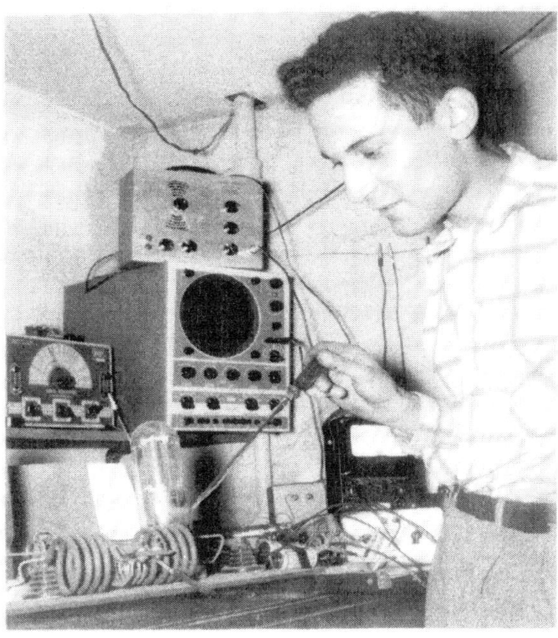

Dominick Lucchesi (1925-1987), was an electronics and radio wizard, as well as pioneer ufologist. Photo from Keller Venus files depicts Lucchesi in early years as scientific consultant for Albert K. Bender's International Flying Saucer Bureau (IFSB), taken sometime in the years of 1952-1953.

"Martians hate Earthlings. They have invaded Earth over and over since the 1890s, but are stopped each time, despite their superior weapons and iron will. Why? Perhaps because they lack the very things they want so much from Earth, warmth and humanity."

—Venusian proverb as told by Dominick C. Lucchesi, pioneer ufologist

Dominick C. Lucchesi (1925-1987) was born and died in Jersey City, New Jersey. Not many researchers in the contemporary UFO community know much about Dominick, other than having some vague recollection of him working closely with Gray Barker, publisher of the Saucerian Press in Clarksburg, West Virginia. Barker, to refresh your memory, popularized the early accounts of the Flatwoods Monster, the notorious Men in Black and the Mothman. Dominick was most well known as an illustrator for many of Barker's unique flying saucer and paranormal publications. His specialty drawings focused on beautiful females, either visitors from the planet Venus or somehow associated with that enigmatic celestial orb.

Dominick had been a UFO investigator since 1952. Together with Gray Barker and fellow New Jersey ufologist August C. Roberts, Dominick was an officer in Albert K. Bender's ill-fated International Flying Saucer Bureau (IFSB) throughout the course of that civilian research organization's brief existence, 1952-1953. It was widely reported that the IFSB was the first civilian UFO research group to be targeted and consequently shut down by the mysterious three "Men in Black." Following the group's demise, Lucchesi and Roberts joined up with James Moseley in founding *Nexus* magazine. This periodical later changed its name to *Saucer News*, whence Barker assumed the duties as editor-in-chief.

A Meeting near Times Square

On Friday, 16 September 1969, Dominick was the featured speaker at a special UFO program sponsored by *Saucer News* and convened in the Hotel Woodstock at 127 West 43rd Street in New York City, not far from Times Square. The title for Dominick's lecture was the, "Philosophy of the Extraterrestrials." Of this meeting, a hand bill proclaimed, "During recent years, Mr. Lucchesi has had several contacts with the Space People, and has gained a deep insight into their philosophy. Over the years he has risen to a position of prominence in one of America's leading aircraft companies- a company which has secret contracts with the government. Therefore, he has understandably been most reluctant to discuss these startling personal experiences, though he has discussed UFO research, in general, on many of Long John Nebel's radio shows in the past."

The "Cosmic Ray" and "North Coast Mike" drive to New York City in September 1969 to attend lecture by multi-talented contactee Dominick Lucchesi.

I was just driving for one year at the time. Having purchased a used 1964 sky-blue, white-topped Pontiac Tempest GTO convertible as my first car with money I earned from working at one of the original double, golden-arched drive-up McDonald's restaurants in Maple Heights, Ohio, and publishing the *Flying Saucer Report*, I had only been on one UFO investigation with Cleveland Ufology Project director Earl J. Neff, driving him up to Detroit, Michigan, in the winter of 1968. There was an individual up there, operating out of a bookstore, claiming to be in contact with Mon-Ka of Mars via mental telepathy; and Neff was trying to determine if this alleged contactee was real or just another fraud duping the UFO community. When the famous Eliot Ness of the Untouchables' fame lived in the Cleveland area during the Great Depression, young Earl Neff served as his sketch artist. So Neff had some experience in law enforcement and transferred some of his skills in this area to his UFO investigative work. In any event, I was so excited to be back on the road again, this time visiting New York City. This would be my initial visit to the Big Apple, but not my last one.

On this trip, however, I was accompanied by Michael A. LaRiche of the popular paranormal talk radio program, *Youth Power*, being broadcast over Cleveland's WZAK -FM station, at 93.1 on the dial. Mike brought his new tape recorder so we wouldn't miss any good tidbits of UFO lore being dispensed by the multi-talented contactee, Dominick Lucchesi.

In the car on the way to New York City, we discussed the forthcoming lecture. "Dominick is a frequent contributor to *Saucer News* as well as to all of the other great work being accomplished by Gray Barker down in Clarksburg," I said to my friend Michael, a.k.a. "North Coast Mike."

"I'm looking forward to his lecture, too, Ray. I brought an extra reel for the recorder, just in case, and extra batteries."

Always fascinated by purported extraterrestrial contacts, I declared that, "I've been impressed by Luchessi's art, but I had no idea that he was actually a contactee as well."

"That's an 'alleged contactee,' Cosmic Ray. Don't get too carried away. Remember what Earl J. Neff always tells us about the so-called contactees. Most of them need to be checked out by the bunko squad.

"Really, Ray, most of these alleged contacts with extraterrestrials from Mars or Venus, or some other planet are very dubious cases. And even if the contact were authentic, how do we know that the so-called 'aliens' are really coming from some other world? Maybe these scenarios are staged by our government or even a foreign power, or perhaps by some nefarious group lurking behind the scenes."

Now, almost fifty years later, I see that Mike had a very good point. In fact, there is a section in my second book of the Venus trilogy, *Final Countdown: Rockets to Venus* (Terra Alta, West Virginia: Headline Books, 2017), where I delve into the possibility that some UFO experiencers may have undergone their close encounters in the confines of a contemporary version of a holodeck, similar to the device depicted on *Star Trek: The Next Generation.* Definitely thinking outside the box, kudos to Mike for his advanced thinking in1969, *Anno Domini*, when most others weren't even considering the possibility that there might be "something" in the UFO phenomenon worthy of consideration, let alone investigating. For a good sense of the zeitgeist of the late sixties and early seventies, please check out my series of articles on the obstacles faced by the late University of Arizona at Tucson physicist, Dr. James E. McDonald, consolidated as a chapter for this book.

Mike called in about a week prior to book a reservation at the hotel. We arrived at the Woodstock around noon. We walked over to the nearby Times Square and bought some dogs and pop from a street vendor. I was delighted that that the hot dogs were covered in genuine New York hot mustard, just like you'd expect to find in Yankee Stadium, the "House that Ruth Built." After inhaling the dogs and pop, we then returned to our room to catch a few winks before going down to the assembly hall about 7:30 p.m. to set up and test the recording equipment.

Dominick was scheduled to begin his lecture promptly at 8:30 p.m. Attendees started filtering in and within thirty minutes of our arrival, the hall was filled to its maximum seating capacity. We could see the lanky Gray Barker, in addition to James Moseley and even Dominick himself fiddling with a projector, wires, microphones and other sound equipment. There were also some unknown individuals setting up tables and spreading out UFO literature for sale from Saucerian Press on them. As crowds gathered around Dominick, interrupting him from his preparatory task of setting up, he kept his composure and gladly signed the programs of all those who approached him. I was duly impressed by his sincere and caring attitude. Seeing that the others were not turned back, Mike and I strolled over to Dominick and introduced ourselves, flashing our credentials. Mine was a press card from the Bedford, Ohio, *Times Register* newspaper, and Mike with a press pass from WZAK radio.

We explained how much we enjoyed his art. I quipped, "You make outer space look a whole lot more interesting than the astronauts do, Mr. Lucchesi."

"So glad you like it, and nice to see so many youth taking an active interest in UFO research," said Dominick. "Say, if you young men have any questions after the show, I would be happy to stick around and answer them."

"That's very kind of you, Mr. Lucchesi. I really appreciate that," said North Coast Mike."

"Thanks, Mr. Lucchesi," added Cosmic Ray, "We're looking forward to interviewing you for the radio program and the *Flying Saucer Report*."

"You can just call me Dom," said the contactee as he shook our hands and then ascended to the dais.

Contact in Stages

During his lecture, Dominick described his contacts with extraterrestrial beings as taking place in stages of increased intensity. In late May 1954, Dominick met a "strange and wonderful person" while visiting a flying saucer club meeting in Paterson, New Jersey. Dominick described this person as a young man, and noted that much of the material that this individual presented to the group "was almost word-for-word" in accordance with the message that he heard delivered by the renowned psychic channel, Meade Layne, when he was out in California during the first week of April for the Interplanetary Spacecraft Convention out at the Landers Field desert airport, less than twenty miles from Yucca Valley.

Dominick did not reveal the speaker's name at the Paterson club meeting. However, he did note that, "This guy didn't say anything about the seismic disturbances; but he did say that the saucer people are our friends and that they could be contacted telepathically." He also added, "They look like us and come from the planet Venus. This person claims to be an adept; and I can vouch for the fact that the 'boy' did have certain powers above and beyond ordinary stuff."

I had the sneaking suspicion that Dominick may have been referring to Howard Menger; but that particular contactee remained largely behind the scenes until about 1957, when he was prominently featured several times on Long John Nebel's *Party Line* radio program, aired late night over a 25-state listening area by Mutual Broadcasting's WOR-AM out of New York City, 710 on the dial. Barker and friends at the Saucerian Press came to call Menger their "boy" because his book, *From Outer Space to You* (1959), was the best-selling of all the literature offered through their Clarksburg office. The only reason that Meade Layne focused on seismic activity and the Paterson speaker did not, so far as I can determine, is that Meade was addressing a largely Southern California audience, to whom earthquakes were always a concern.

Rob Potter of the Promise Revealed meets Commander Aura Rhanes in the Cheat Lake, West Virginia, Public Library, on 20 November 2019.

Enter the "Space Girl"

It is clear that the anonymous Paterson speaker's lecture inspired Dominick to think about the possibility of Venusians not only visiting our planet in their flying saucers, but actually living and working among us clandestinely. Dominick tried as he could to telepathically focus his thoughts skyward, hoping to summon a Venusian into his life. Being of Italian-Sicilian descent, he believed that his ancestors were in direct contact with the Venusians. He often related legends from the days of the great Roman Empire when sky gods from Venus, arriving in our atmosphere in their motherships, would deploy their "flying shields" and descend to the surface of the Earth. As they strode the Earth and exhibited amazing powers, the people throughout the Roman Empire worshipped them as gods. Some Earthlings were chosen to be paired with these divine beings. Trusted with the keys to Venusian advanced technology, their hybrid children would bring further light and knowledge to the future generations of humankind.

This thought constantly raced through Dominick's head: "Perhaps the gods never left."

Illustration below: "Lady Venus, Space Commander" by Dominick Lucchesi, as cover for the October 1954 issue of *Nexus* magazine, Vol. 4, Tome 1.

Dominick Lucchesi believed that the gods of ancient Rome were Venusian cosmonauts.

Photo from Keller Venus files depicts Dominick Lucchesi as a frequent guest on Long John Nebel's Party Line program, broadcast nightly from New York City to a listening area covering 25 states over the WOR Radio, Mutual Broadcasting Company's transmitter at 710 on the AM dial. While Lucchesi did not hesitate to discuss many UFO cases he had personally investigated, he was reluctant to reveal his own experiences as a contactee.

Beginning with Albert K. Bender's International Flying Saucer Bureau (IFSB), back in 1952-1953, Dominick Lucchesi cut his teeth as a certified flying saucer investigator. All of the way up to his death in 1987, Dominick never declined an opportunity to check out any report of a close encounter with UFOs and/or their occupants.

One of the most unusual cases he investigated involved the landing of a small saucer outside of Peekskill, New York, on 20 February 1954. Concerning this report, Dominick read from his notebook's "personal file" entry dated 23 February 1954: "Was informed of sighting by Mr. Jack Forster's brother-in-law on February 23rd, 1954. He informed me that sister (Irene) was sick and nervous due to a severe shock incurred Saturday while she and her husband went to New York State to examine property. He could not enlighten me as to the nature of the phenomenon, but said that his sister mentioned something about seeing an odd and weird creature or something of that nature."

On the following day, Dominick went to visit Mr. Forster and hinted to him that he was curious as to the nature of the phenomenon seen by his wife and himself; and that perhaps he could he could assimilate the evidence into a more or less practical explanation. Dominick noted that, "I had no inkling at the time that flying objects were involved, but thought that it was my chance to investigate occult phenomenon at close hand, or something to that effect."

Keeping in mind that most people in the first half of the 1950s were quite skeptical of UFO reports, and the subject of life on other planets generally, Dominick declared that, "Mr. Forster informed me that he would not consent to telling me what had transpired unless I promised not to reveal his address, as he did not want to face the derision that would come his way were his friends and relatives to find out."

An Astounding Narrative Unfolds

Dominick tape recorded Jack Forster's narrative and played it for those in attendance:

"My wife and I drove up to Peekskill. That's where I am going to build a summer home. Upon arriving at the entrance to a dirt trail that leads to my property, I pulled the car off the highway; and she and I began to walk toward the rear of the acreage which is all wooded and extends about 300 yards, and then drops off in a steep bank before continuing to the slope of the mountain or hill.

"We walked around for a while; and before we knew it, it was starting to get dark. You know the way it gets before it really darkens! Well, anyway, we were about a mile in from the highway when we started back; and Irene called my attention to a gleam showing between the trees.

"I would say now that I think back, that it was about 200 yards away and very faint, as the trees were blocking a clear view of it. I was in an exceptionally good mood and very calm or absent-minded, you know, in the way you get sometimes; and I like a darn fool, I started to walk toward the gleam, sort of unthinking like. At about a hundred feet or so, we rounded a big rock. Well, I mean, I don't quite know how to put it. You're going to think I'm nuts, or something.

"Well, anyway, I saw it. It gleamed like, brassy, sort of; and it-she, well, anyway, something was standing on the side or deck of this thing. It was a girl and I'm sure; and so is Irene."

Jack Describes the Spacecraft

Dominick tape recorded Jack Forster's testimony only three days following the encounter. It was clear in the recording that Jack's voice remained highly animated and excited as he, along with his wife, bore witness of the girl from outer space.

Jack Forster continued, "For a few moments, I think my mind went blank or numb, or something; as I did not feel myself get frightened. I tried to study the thing, I mean girl, and tried to get a look into the thing as the port or door was opened. It seemed hazy or misty inside. All I could see was a few glass-like rods with bluish balls or spheres on the ends. It looked like high frequency stuff, you know, that sort of thing pretty well. Well, anyway, I saw some black piping and stuff, too. The outside of the thing, the top part anyway, was brassy colored and looked dimpled or hammered-like; and the bottom had that funny gleam like stainless steel, dull and shiny at the same time. Pipes came out of the bottom of the top, if you can understand that, and went down to the edge of the thing. I guess like all technicians, I was more interested in the mechanism than the creature or girl."

Were the illuminated glass rods a type of fiber optic cables? Was the description of "high frequency" equipment indicative of some advanced type of electro-magnetic propulsion? Remember that this encounter took place in early 1954; so the description of a not yet invented fiber optic technology adds credence to the report, in my opinion.

Exotic "Space Girl"

It figures. Jack, ever the quintessential nerd, paid more attention to the vehicle than its hot female, extraterrestrial pilot. Nevertheless, the technically-minded contactee finally got around to providing Dominick with his impressions of the exotic "Space Girl."

"It was a girl all right," emphasized Jack, adding that, "I'm sure of that." He further explained that, "She seemed to have a black, rubber hood that extended half-way down her back. It seemed to be inflated. I could see it pulse or change size. She had a tube that went in the port in one hand, and a black box with a wire in the other. There was a plastic-like mask over her face, and a goggle-like thing. They were like all one piece.

"I don't know if it was my imagination, or what, but her eyes seemed luminous as they shined through the darkish glass of the goggles pretty clear at about that time the realization hit me. I began to shake like a leaf. My wife was gripping my hand so tight that it hurt like anything; and she seemed rooted to the spot. When I pulled her to get the heck away from there, she was stiff like a board and wouldn't move. I had to yank and shake her to get her out of there and back to the car.

"I drove about three miles and stopped. I was worried about the wife. She was white as a sheet; and her mouth was moving; but she couldn't talk. The reason I stopped was that my feet and legs were shaking so much that I couldn't drive right. I waited a few minutes and had a smoke. That calmed me a little. I started for home and stopped once to get Irene some coffee. I think she's still shaking from it; and its a few days since it happened, too.

Jack Forster wrapped up his account. "That's about all. I know it sounds funny; and I guess you think I'm really gone. I only told you because you believe some pretty crazy stuff yourself. Besides, I think you might have an idea what and where it came from.

"Here's my wife now! Irene, Irene, come tell Dommie here what you saw!"

Irene Forster stepped up to the microphone, only adding a small detail here and there. Dominick noted that, "Mr. and Mrs. Forster sat with me and described in detail over and over again until my sketch was as close to what they saw as possible. After I put the final touches on the sketch for the Forsters, Jack blurted out, "It's too damn close! Are you sure you never saw one, Dommie?"

There was an extended pause on the tape. Then you hear Dominick's only, but faint comment, "Wish I did."

Of course, not wanting to alarm the Forsters anymore than they already were, there was a lot of information that Dominick had gathered about flying saucers and their occupants that he was keeping to himself.

Additional Details Explain Lucchesi's Drawing

As the tape rolled on and continued to record, missing details of the encounter and description of the Space Girl were coming to light as Jack and Irene Forster guided Dominick Lucchesi while his sketch was in the very process of being drawn.

For the benefit of the readers, it was revealed that the Space Girl's clothes seemed to be of a gray, metallic mesh. The girl was approximately five- feet tall, give or take a couple of inches, but well proportioned. There also appeared to be a very fine, hazy plastic suit covering the figure. It looked like cellophane and extended about three inches from the body, probably inflated. A brassy belt, or girdle, encircled the waist, and a wide brassy bracelet high on the left arm above the elbow. The fingers of the creature or girl seemed to be excessively supple, as Jack stated that he thought he saw them bend the wrong way. Jack was not sure of this point, however, and said that the strange lighting may have served to create this effect. The place of the event was also examined. It indicated that a heavy oval object was there.

Below: First generation ufologist Jim Moseley was so impressed with Jack and Irene Forster's close encounter that he used Dominick Lucchesi's drawing of the "Space Girl" to illustrate the cover of the December 1954 issue of the innovative *Nexus* magazine, the precursor to *Saucer News*.

"Pilot of the Airwaves, this is my request…."

From Keller Venus Files: As a ham radio operator, Dominick Lucchesi would mail out his QSL card to distant short wave listeners. You never know who may be tuning in.

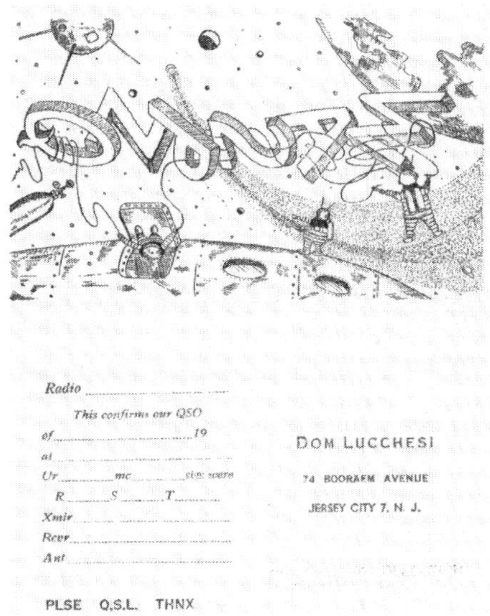

From Keller Venus Files: Dominick could summon the beautiful Space Girl with an emergency signal watch powered by a Cytherium crystal activation device.

One can understand Dominick Lucchesi's obsession with extraterrestrial women. The various contactee accounts that most captured his fancy were those that struck some resonance in his personal life. Dominick experienced real encounters with female emissaries of other worlds. Although it took him 15 years to come out with it, in his own words, the early experiencer recounted his very first such episode at the UFO convention convened in New York City's Woodstock Hotel on the evening of 16 September 1969, attended by the Cosmic Ray and North Coast Mike in their early years as flying saucer investigators from the Greater Cleveland, Ohio, area.

In Dominick Lucchesi's Own Words
Revelations from Outer Space: A True and Startling Tale

On the night of 17 January 1954, I was contacted by an amateur radio operator who resides in the immediate vicinity of my home. The nature of the contact was to the effect that in experimenting with higher frequency receivers, the ham radio operator had decided to utilize a radical new antenna designed by my brother Frank for the purposes of power reception and transmission.

It was my neighbor's idea that by using the antenna for the purpose of the reception of signals, he could amplify incoming signals to tremendous proportions, thereby increasing the otherwise limited range of the receiver. He stated that he had carried out this experiment in an odd manner. First, he had connected the antenna by a switch circuit to the incoming leads so that he could, by the throw of a switch, introduce the new antenna into the circuit. This would enable him to compare the signal values, or difference between the two.

Having completed his hook-up, he switched to normal antenna and began to tune the higher frequency bands, watching his signal meter flick slightly as it began to pick up slight disturbances on a band that was in the ultra-high frequency range. Out of curiosity, he switched in the new antenna and was amazed to hear a voice emanating from the speaker while the signal meter pegged on full stop. He claimed the voice to spoke to him, as if it knew he could hear it. The voice said, "You are in proper resonance. Do not change your settings."

Becoming frightened, he cut the switch on and off in a flurry of indecision. Then calming a little, he sat to listen. It was a few minutes before the voice resumed. It said, "Contact someone who can understand.... Space...."

Static interference blocked the reception between the words. "....far.... distant.... Do not turn receiver off.... Contact.... Someone who will understand.... Space.... Velocity interferes with frequency.... Contact.... Now....down soon near.... Wait.... Switch.... Resonates.... or....contact our unit...."

The receiver went silent and the signal meter skipped to zero. Putting on his jacket, he ran to my house and told me this story. My curiosity aroused, I went with him to his home and radio room. I sat in silence as he told me over and over that it really happened. I looked at the receiver that was still turned on and picked up the pad on which he had taken down the message. Putting together the words of the message, "Switch....Resonates," and feeling a little foolish as I did so, I began to send by flipping the on and off switch of the receiver in Morse code. I sent the following: -.-. --- -. - .- -.-. - .... . .- .- over and over, "Contact hear---- Contact hear----- -. --- .— Now---- Now." Then, leaving the switch on, I sat back and waited, looking frequently at the sweep hand on my watch.

After about twelve minutes, the mater needle flicked to full scale and a voice emanated from the speaker. Quickly picking up pad and pencil, I took down the message. The voice had a slight alien accent that was like nothing I ever heard before. I believe it sounded slightly Asiatic in intonation, but can't be sure. This is the message in its entirety:

"You are Contact Seven----- You are Contact Seven-------- Hear! Hear! Do not turn receiver off---------- Do not turn receiver off---- Static---- (interference for about 30 seconds, then message resumes).

"Listen close---- Listen close—Listen close---------- We will be seen if you follow main highway westward...." There was a repetition of the same message several times.

At this point, the voice began to get clearer, as it continued: "Be on highway in exactly 16 minutes--- 16 minutes---- 16 minutes. Stop vehicle near swampland---- Stop vehicle near swampland---- look toward sky westward----- Look toward sky westward----- follow, follow, follow, follow to destination........ Blue glow---- Blue glow...." This message was repeated in its entirety three times.

The message continued with, "----------Now, Now, Now, Now, Now," which faded into nothing as the meter slowly returned to zero signal.

Looking at my companion Vince to see his reaction, I asked what he thought of the message. He was at a complete loss of words. The only highway I knew of that aimed westward through swampland was S3. Figuring to follow the strange occurrence to its end, I told Vince that he should put on his jacket and come along. We arrived at the middle point where the highway intersects the New Jersey swamps about a mile past the Hackensack River. In exactly 12 minutes, and looking westward over the peaks of the Orange Mountains, we searched the sky for a blue, glowing object.

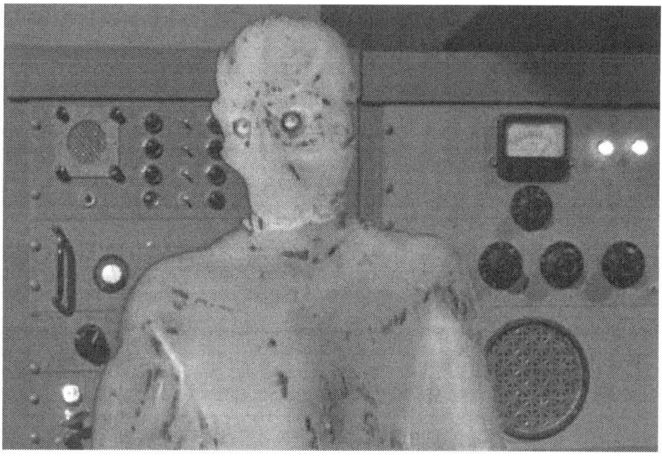

The first episode of the *Outer Limits* television program, broadcast on the evening of 16 September 1963, featured the "Galaxy Being," an electro-magnetic entity accidentally brought down to Earth from the Andromeda star cluster as a radio engineer was using a small California town's commercial station's KXKVI facilities to research microwave background radiation in outer space and capture some of it in his own invention of a three dimensional television set. The galaxy being was not satisfied with staying put in the "boob tube," however, and decided to take a tour of the Central Valley environs, accidentally killing a few people with lethal doses of cosmic rays. Some of the contactees in the 1950s and 1960s, to include Dominick Lucchesi, claimed to first contact extraterrestrials via ham radio sets. One has to wonder if Leslie Stevens, the author of the "Galaxy Being," was inspired by such amazing accounts as provided by Lucchesi? Photo is from archives of United Artists, Los Angeles, California.

While wondering if the message had been interpreted correctly, it was Vince who first noticed the glow; and I had to follow his pointing finger to find it. I estimated its distance as about three miles by noticing the slight cloud formation which it had penetrated. It was extremely faint; and had I not known where to look, I would have missed it entirely. Occasionally, it would flicker out for about 15 seconds and would appear again.

By this time, I was driving along the highway, maintaining a steady speed of fifty miles per hour, without realizing we had traveled 45 miles and were on U.S. Route 6 in the vicinity of Hackettstown. An abrupt change of direction of the object forced us to turn into a secondary road southward; and we found ourselves in an isolated district with an occasional farm breaking the landscape. Having been in the general area once before, I thought we were in the Schoolboy Mountain area.

Suddenly, the object glowed brighter and began to grow in size. I could not tell whether it was stationary and we were moving toward it, or if it was moving toward us. A loud humming vibration filled my ears. I could even feel the car vibrate in unison. Without realizing I had turned into a dirt road that was overgrown with weeds, and coming to an opening in the trees, I turned off my headlights. I then waited for my eyes to become accustomed to the darkness. Continuing to repent of the fact that I had no flashlight, I became cognizant that by this time Vince was begging me to turn back. He was even trying to push me away from the driver's seat. Fearing that he would leave, I took the keys out of the ignition and stepped out into the high grass. Suddenly, I was overcome by a feeling of intense and insatiable curiosity which overcame all traces of fear. I walked toward the field in which the object seemed to settle.

My eyes gradually accustomed themselves to the darkness as I pushed aside the brushes and weeds. And then my hair stood on end; and I froze momentarily. My throat constricted, for something stood in the center of the path, blocking my way. I overcame the momentary panic. My own pride would not allow me to show fear. I did not know whether to say something ridiculously outrageous or ridiculously common. My mind was flowing like a kaleidoscope.

I heard myself say, "Who are you?" The figure turned about and started to walk away from me. A strong compulsion made me follow and all fear left. It was supplanted by a feeling of resignation to whatever may follow. I guess I was tired. I don't know.

After walking about 25 yards, I saw the dim outline of an egg-shaped structure with an open port in its side that gleamed dimly with a fluorescent cast. Limned in the light, the figure I followed took on a more normal appearance. I saw it was a man in a loose fitting coverall tied at the ankles and wrists. On his head, he had a tight-fitting, skin tight helmet with small projections on the ear flaps, like tiny hearing aid buttons. He walked straight into the craft without even turning around.

I was momentarily interrupted in my observations. Vinnie run up and grasped my wrist from behind, trying to pull me away from the thing. I do not remember the remark I said to him, but let go and stood beside me quietly as the realization of the series of events struck him.

He said, "What should we do now?"

Without answering and fearing I would have to act now, I ran for the open port and walked into the craft. I estimated its size and construction as about fifty feet in length and ovoid in shape, with no rivets or external projections being apparent, except for a band or rim about four feet in width and two feet in thickness. It was circling the outer part of the hull. There were large squares spaced along this rim, whose outer surface looked like a metallic mosaic, like a photo cell. I made the mistake, however, of touching the sides of the port with my hands and recoiled at the slight electric charge of the hull.

The floor deck inside the port was of non-reflective, dull black composition that felt like sponge rubber, but with such a smooth surface that I sensed it was not. I noticed that the port was in actuality an airlock; and passing through a second port, I found myself in a circular room with a grilled round lamp shining down from the domed ceiling.

My senses, for some reason, were acutely sharp. A buzzing noise, like a swarm of bees, emanated from the ceiling fixture. I felt my whole body tingling from inside out. I felt slightly lighter, for some reason. I went and touched the walls. They were smooth like glass, but non-reflecting. The construction did not seem as alien as it seemed advanced. That's the only way I could phrase it.

In the middle of the floor there was an upright cylinder that seemed to be rotating slowly, descending about seven feet from the ceiling overhead. When it came to a stop, a door slid open from the top. It beckoned me to step into it, which I did. The door closed and the cylinder, which apparently was an elevator, carried me to an upper deck. I found myself in what appeared to be a control room.

There were two men sitting at the control chairs. They turned around and smiled in a friendly manner. One of them waved his arm in a gesture. It seemed that he wanted me to sit near the panel with him. I did so and noticed the simplicity of the panel before me. There was a large screen in front of the two men that had lines moving along it, like an oscilloscope in a radio shop. The panels were inlaid with small knobs and buttons. There were no switches and levers in the whole cabin.

I was startled to see a female walk in. She sat at one of the panels. She was dressed in a gray coverall, differing only in color to the ones the men were wearing. I did not know whether to speak or remain quite. I tried to observe any strange physical characteristic. I noticed the men's necks were heavily muscled and corded. They were wiry in build; and for their size, seemed extremely strong. It was the eyes that had the oddness of appearance, an oddness I could not define.

I began to get jumpy at the silence; and at the same time, did not want to be the one to break it.

Contact with the "Space Girl"

The girl must have sensed my discomfort. Walking over to another panel, she removed a transparent chart from an illuminated surface and handed it to me. Immediately after she picked up the chart, a shaded but honeycombed impression momentarily formed on the panel's surface, but then quickly re-illuminated. The chart seemed similar to celluloid; but when bent, it would not crack or tear.

The diagram had a maze of lines and figures on it. Instinct told me it was a chart of sorts; but I could not recognize the form of writing. Nevertheless, there were a number of the configurations that were similar to ours. I felt a light touch on my shoulder. I turned around to notice another girl smiling at me in amused observation.

She said, "Your friend awaits you outside. I spoke to him; but he refused to enter our conveyance. The other three do not know your tongue. It was for that reason they did not speak."

I noted that her voice was emotionless, yet friendly. She wore a garment similar to a sun suit. Her hair fell to her shoulders like a page-boy hairdo. Her eyes were intensely alive. On her head rested a red beret with a diamond-studded, golden bee pin.

I spoke to her in a statement. I said, "This is a spacecraft."

She acknowledged with a nod. I asked, "Why did you contact us?" She shrugged and told me that their sensitive receivers had indicated a circuit which was in tune electrically with their transmission apparatus and decided that it deserved consideration. Upon my asking why they had come to the planet Earth, she answered with the fact that they (she and her crew) were to their civilization what our explorers and scientists are to our culture.

I fumbled in my jacket pocket for the pad and pencil I had taken from Vinnie's radio bench. I held them up to her with a questioning glance. She nodded her head in approval and answered the following questions without hesitation, and in extreme patience. I wondered if now, that I had the supreme opportunity, I could ask the right questions. What was paramount in my mind? Everything had seemed to lose perspective and value. My very senses reeled under the implications.

Dominick Lucchesi sketched his own version of Commander Aura Rhanes based on his personal encounter with her along with the description provided him by California contactee Truman Bethurum. The original sketch is located in the Gray Barker Collection in Clarksburg, West Virginia, and was reproduced with permission along with a lengthy account of the Commander's activities, on page 71 of my epic book, *Cosmic Ray's Excellent Venus Adventure* (Terra Alta, WV: Headline Books), 2017. All the Venus books are fully illustrated throughout and available on amazon.com while supplies last.

As if in a dream, I acted. These are the questions I asked. It is for you, the believers and the unbelievers, to judge as to whether they were the proper ones or the wrong ones. What would you have done? What would you have asked?

The "Q and A" Session

Q. What is your name and where are you from?

A. My name is Captain Aura Rhanes and I am from the planet you know as Venus.

Q. What is the driving force of this craft?

A. The only way I could describe it in your tongue would be to state that it is an electro-dynamic turbine. However, I do not think you would understand fully how it operates.

Q. What is the name of your ship and what is its purpose?

A. Our ship is called the *Spartacus*. It is a scientific exploration vessel.

Q. Do the Earth governments have a vehicle similar to yours?

A. Yes, they have one, but only in general outline. The underlying principles are common; but your present level of technology is, as yet, too impractical for implementation.

Q. Do you have a base on the planet Earth? If so, could you tell me where?

A. We have several on the Earth, as well as the side of the Moon that you cannot observe from the surface of your world. There are bases in Antarctica and some areas of South America, as well as under your larger and deeper bodies of water.

Q. Does your government intend to invade any of the nations of Earth?

A. We do not have a type of government that you would readily understand. While we will not invade any of your nations, we will work clandestinely to see that any dangers directed towards us are averted.

Q. What is wrong with the human race, as it is known?

A. The humans do not think in a logical manner. They are quite emotional. Environmental conditioning and educational standards remain at the lowest order. Your teachers, for the most part, are no more intelligent than their pupils, at least as far as the whole conceptualization of the interplay between mind and logic is concerned.

Q. What is the best way to gain knowledge?

A. Knowledge may best be gained through its transmission by telepathic means, initiated by someone who knows how this is properly done and can assist the receiver in their development of cumulative memory channels.

Q. Do we have to accept things on faith?

A. There should be no such emotion as faith. It retards progress in the logic-mind-matter-energy–reaction, thus creating a barrier toward further thoughts on any specific trend one is pursuing. But saying this, I still have to admire the humans for their capacity to be inspired by it, to even risk their own lives if they fervently believe in something. That is the mark of a true revolutionary, to even die for the people, if necessary.

Living with the Humans

Q. Have you ever lived amongst Earth people?

A. Yes. But few and far between are the encounters we enjoy with men and women of Earth who possess a mind that is at the same time both exhilarating and progressive, in conjunction with our own.

Q. Do you enjoy physical contact with the opposite sex?

A. Yes.

Q. Well, isn't that an emotion?

A. I wouldn't say that it was an emotion in the manner that you are thinking, right at this moment. But it is a sense, much like pain, sight, smell, etc. There is a definite sense of physical feeling, but not emotional, as Earth people think. We're not into all the drama you humans attach to it.

Q. I'm not sure I catch where you are going with that answer. Could you clarify this for me?

A. At this moment, Dominick, you were thinking in terms of the physical sense-love-contact. Eliminate the love and you have, well, sense-contact. Love is the term you people have used to rationalize a number of physical-mental senses that you are unable to isolate separately, and in their entirety to the whole of the logic-mental-concept.

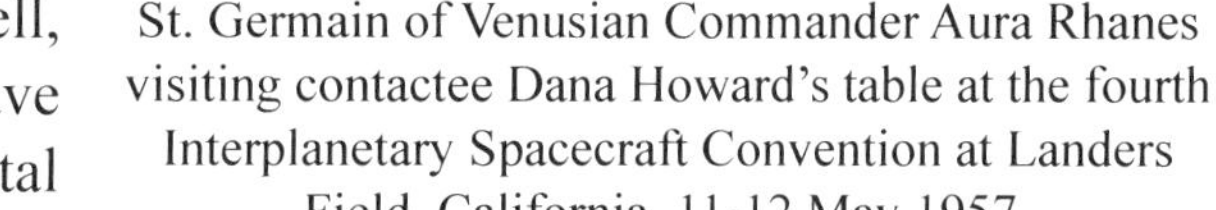
From Dr. Keller's "Venus Files," here is the full frame of photos taken by New York attorney Jules B. St. Germain of Venusian Commander Aura Rhanes visiting contactee Dana Howard's table at the fourth Interplanetary Spacecraft Convention at Landers Field, California, 11-12 May 1957.

Q. Then you are recommending that human race should not love?

A. I want you to understand the full array of senses that you term love; and then utilize these senses and you will arrive at something much better than the term you use to describe the conglomerate sensations that you term love.

Q. Do you consider, then, that these questions I am asking are of a low order, or even childish in some sense?

A. No, not at all; but they are the natural questions that would be asked by a person at your point of mental evolution, one who has explored the progressive thought concept.

Q. In what way do you attempt to accomplish this?

A. Collectively speaking, we accomplish this by living logically and attempting to impart our knowledge to lower orders of celestial life. Of course, in doing this, we can only divulge information that the particular beings in question are capable of assimilating in an intelligent and progressive manner.

Q. What is the average human intelligence rating?

A. In attempting to answer your question, I would require a complete census of the many intelligences found inhabiting this and other universes. Of course, were you to ask what your inherent intelligence rating may be, we can safely state that you are above the lower order in many ways, but in the higher orders ranking only in various phases of intellectual progressiveness.

Q. How does our philosophy differ from yours?

A. Philosophy, as you call it, is nothing but the effort of your minds working in conjunction with your ego and foolish emotional facilities attempting to prove and deceive yourselves into thinking that you are able to assimilate and propound knowledge of cosmic proportions; when in actuality, it is not practical nor progressive to attempt to understand a concept of proportions that your finite minds cannot follow.

Q. Can you propound one of these concepts?

A. I will attempt to answer your question to the best of my ability. First, you must understand that mere words do not convey the actual thought concepts of the individual. They only stir the mind and imagination of the persons who hear or read these words, so that they may interpret them in their own way of thought formation. The only way that a person can convey a mental concept is through the power of telepathic communication. Why should a person strive to understand the infinite, when he or she is finite? A person should strive to understand the mind only to the extent or term of.... a mind-time cycle of existence, and not beyond, as that is useless to the mind itself.

Really, you Earthlings have the foolish idea that it is possible to convey actual concepts by word pictures. Yet, everyone through thinking of the same thing would visualize the actuality differently in their own mind. Think back to your own Plato and his story of the shadows on the cave wall.

Science fiction or fact?

Evelyn E. Smlth's bibliography

Throughout the 1950s, Evelyn E. Smith regularly published science fiction in magazines like Galaxy and Fantastic Universe. Her stories ranged from adventures to post-apocalyptic satires. What she was most noted for, however, was dealing with questions of gender identity. Like all of her work, these novels are characterized by their sharp wit. Goodreads declares that, "At her best, she was the equal of anyone -- male or female -- writing for the pulp magazines."

Some of her more notable science fiction stories include:

TEA TRAY IN THE SKY
NOT FIT FOR CHILDREN
COLLECTOR'S ITEM
THE DOORWAY
THE VILBAR PARTY
HELPFULLY YOURS
THE VENUS TRAP
THE MOST SENTIMENTAL MAN
ONCE A GREECH
THE BLUE TOWER
MY FAIR PLANET
SENTRY IN THE SKY

When not breaking glass ceilings in the male-dominated science fiction universe, Evelyn was commanding the Venusian space base Clarion on the far side of the Moon and piloting the Spartacus patrol ship to monitor the military activities of the space powers here on Earth.

Evelyn opines on exotic Venus

"What's the matter, darling?" James asked anxiously. "Don't you like the planet?"

"Oh, I love the planet," Phyllis said. "It's beautiful."

It was. The blue--really blue--grass, blue-violet shrubbery and, loveliest of all, the great golden tree with sapphire leaves and pale pink blossoms, instead of looking alien, resembled nothing so much as a fairy-tale version of Earth.

Even the fragrance that filled the atmosphere was completely delightful to Terrestrial nostrils -- which was unusual, for most other planets, no matter how well adapted for colonization otherwise, tended, from the human viewpoint, anyway, to stink. Not that they were not colonized nevertheless, for the population of Earth was expanding at too great a rate to permit merely olfactory considerations to rule out an otherwise suitable planet. This particular group of settlers had been lucky, indeed.

-Excerpted from THE VENUS TRAP, Galaxy sci-fi magazine, June 1956

Significance of Radio Communications in Flying Saucer Encounters

Rare photo snapped by Dominick Lucchesi from Keller Venus Files depicts renowned anthropologist and archaeologist Dr. George Hunt Williamson descending from the dais at the First Interplanetary Spacecraft Convention held at Giant Rock, Landers Field, California, on Sunday, 4 April 1954. Lucchesi attended the convention on behalf of the Nexus flying saucer magazine.

What is highly significant about Lucchesi's case is that it was facilitated by direct radio communications from a Venusian saucer pilot. Interestingly, contemporary radio astronomers utilize huge interstellar dishes or vast arrays of smaller radio telescopes linked to a central computerized network in the hope of finding and communicating with intelligent beings on other distant worlds or even in other dimensions lying outside our own space-time continuum. All of these unprecedented efforts come at a great cost to the taxpayers of many countries. While the discovery of radio transmissions directed to Earth by some distant outer space civilization would be a momentous event, and one that would ultimately justify the cost of the project's public funding, a few researchers, both concerned scientists and interested ufologists, have speculated that perhaps extraterrestrials or ultra-dimensional beings, operating their craft in the vicinity of our planet, have already beamed sundry electronic communications to various contacts right here. This may have been going on since the very invention of radio. In my first book in the *Venus Rising* series, I elaborate on the early radio experiments and alleged extraterrestrial communications received by the electronics wizard, Nikola Tesla (b. 1856), beginning in the year 1898 and up through his death in 1943. Tesla claims that via his own invention of the so-called "Tesla-Scope," he was in direct radio communication with super scientific civilizations on both Mars and Venus.

***

Also, just two years before Lucchesi's own extraterrestrial experiences, the renowned Arizona-based pioneer astro-archaeologist, Dr. George Hunt Williamson (1926-1986), was claiming that he was in "off-and-on again" radio communications with the occupants of a flying saucer from Venus. Williamson was also noted as being one of the witnesses to the master of the mystic arts George Adamski's encounter with a Venusian saucer pilot named Orthon at Desert Center, California, on 20 November 1952. Williamson drew a sketch of Orthon as being a beautiful young woman. This was subsequently published in the 4 December 1954 issue of *Valor: The Magazine of Soulcraft*, headquartered in Noblesville, Indiana. This astounding sketch has also been reproduced in my book, *Final Countdown: Rockets to Venus* (Terra Alta, West Virginia: Headline Books, 2017).

He also took plaster casts of the extraterrestrial's footprints, and forwarded these to a Livermore Laboratories physicist using the alias of "Peter Kor," in December 1956. Kor, in a letter to Gray Barker of the Saucerian Press in Clarksburg, West Virginia, described the footprints as being from a small, size-6 shoe with rather indistinct markings. On Sunday, 17 June 2018, Northeast Ohio UFO investigator, Michael A. LaRiche, and I drove out to Mr. Kor's home in the Greater Cleveland area and asked him about the footprints. Kor, now in his late 80s but in a very spry condition, noted that one of the footprints broke in half sometime *en route* to his home, after it was mailed from Dr. Williamson's residence in Prescott, Arizona. Kor kept the footprints for three months before Dr.Williamson asked for them back; and he dutifully returned them. Unfortunately, he did not take any photographs of them while they were in his possession. Soon after the footprints were back in Dr. Williamson's custody, the anthropologist-archaeologist set off for Peru in an attempt to discover evidence for the presence of ancient astronauts that once inhabited the western cordillera of South America, the Andes Mountains range.

"Did the footprints appear to be made from the imprint of a small woman's or a girl's shoe?" I inquired. "Yes, they did," said Kor. He also explained that Adamski and Dr. Williamson had been corresponding with him when he was writing for various publications of Raymond A. Palmer such as *Amazing Stories, Fate, Mystic* and *Search* in the late 1940s and early 1950s, before the famous encounter at Desert Center. He invited the two most well-known saucer experiencers and researchers of the age to come up to Cleveland and present some lectures. Adamski and Dr. Williamson took Kor up on his offer and met for the first time right before they addressed a maximum capacity crowd of 500 in a downtown Cleveland hotel for an event promoted well ahead by Kor in conjuction with local research groups, the Cleveland UFO Society and the Cleveland Ufology Project. Kor described Adamski as a "true mystic at heart" and Dr. Williamson as a "bright-eyed and bushy-tailed researcher, a true seeker."

Peter Kor, first generation ufologist and columnist for Raymond Palmer's esoteric publications (L) with Dr. Raymond Keller (R), author of the Venus Rising Trilogy, in Mr. Kor's Northeast Ohio home, on 17 June 2018. Photo was taken by Michael LaRiche.

At the same time that Dr. Williamson was asserting that he was talking with Venusians via a ham radio set, the United States Air Force established a TOP SECRET program code-named MQ707, the purpose of which was to establish telecommunications with highly advanced extraterrestrials in the hope of coaxing them to land one of their ships at Edwards Air Force Base in California. This was to take place on a certain date and time where President Dwight D. Eisenhower could clear his schedule, fly out to California and meet the flying saucer occupants in person.

At the From Venus with Love conference, sponsored by Rob Potter's thepromiserevealed.com and which was held on the slopes of Mt. Shasta from 27-29 July 2018, I revealed much more concerning Peter Kor and his connections with George Adamski and Dr. George Hunt Williamson, replete with some amazing photographs both current and past, harkening back to those early days of the contactee era.

From Keller Venus Files-Williamson: Letter from "Peter Kor" to Gray Barker, dated 8 December 1956 (L) with reply letter from Saucerian Press publisher Gray Barker to Kor dated 12 December 1956 (R). The writers of these letters consider the matter of Orthon's footprints, as captured in plaster casts made by Dr. George Hunt Williamson out in Mojave Desert on 20 November 1952, the date of George Adamski's first physical contact with the Venusians.

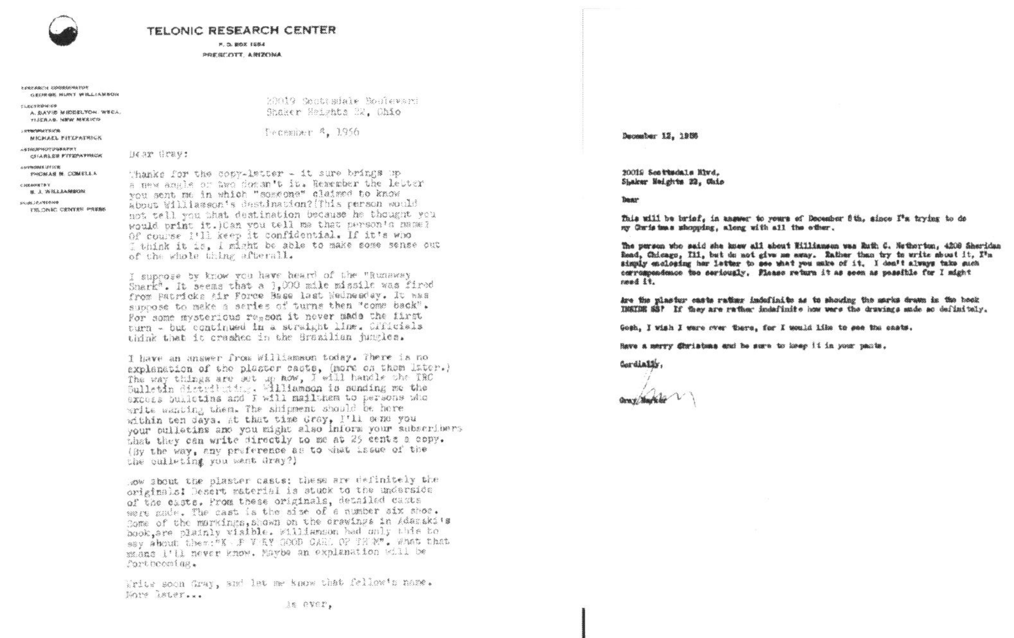

TELONIC RESEARCH CENTER
P. O. BOX 1684
PRESCOTT, ARIZONA

RESEARCH COORDINATOR GEORGE HUNT WILLIAMSON
ELECTRONICS A. DAVID MIDDELTON, WECA, TIJERAS, NEW MEXICO
MICHAEL FITZPATRICK
ASTROPHOTOGRAPHY CHARLES FITZPATRICK
THOMAS M. COMELLA
CHEMISTRY B. J. WILLIAMSON
PUBLICATIONS TELONIC CENTER PRESS

20019 Scottsdale Boulevard
Shaker Heights 22, Ohio

December 8, 1956

Dear Gray:

Thanks for the copy-letter - it sure brings up a new angle or two doesn't it. Remember the letter you sent me in which "someone" claimed to know about Williamson's destination?(This person would not tell you that destination because he thought you would print it.)Can you tell me that person's name? Of course I'll keep it confidential. If it's who I think it is, I might be able to make some sense out of the whole thing afterall.

I suppose by know you have heard of the "Runaway Snark". It seems that a 3,000 mile missile was fired from Patricks Air Force Base last Wednesday. It was suppose to make a series of turns then "come back". For some mysterious reason it never made the first turn - but continued in a straight line. Officials think that it crashed in the Brazilian jungles.

I have an answer from Williamson today. There is no explanation of the plaster casts, (more on them later.) The way things are set up now, I will handle the TRC Bulletin distributing. Williamson is sending me the excess bulletins and I will mail them to persons who write wanting them. The shipment should be here within ten days. At that time Gray, I'll send you your bulletins and you might also inform your subscribers that they can write directly to me at 25 cents a copy. (By the way, any preference as to what issue of the the bulleting you want Gray?)

Now about the plaster casts: these are definitely the originals! Desert material is stuck to the underside of the casts. From these originals, detailed casts were made. The cast is the size of a number six shoe. Some of the markings,shown on the drawings in Adamski's book,are plainly visible. Williamson had only this to say about them:"KEEP VERY GOOD CARE OF THEM". What that means I'll never know. Maybe an explanation will be forthcoming.

Write soon Gray, and let me know that fellow's name. More later...

As ever,

December 12, 1956

20019 Scottsdale Blvd.
Shaker Heights 22, Ohio

Dear

This will be brief, in answer to yours of December 8th, since I'm trying to do my Christmas shopping, along with all the other.

The person who said she knew all about Williamson was Ruth C. Netherton, 4200 Sheridan Road, Chicago, Ill, but do not give me away. Rather than try to write about it, I'm simply enclosing her letter to see what you make of it. I don't always take such correspondence too seriously. Please return it as soon as possible for I might need it.

Are the plaster casts rather indefinite as to showing the marks drawn in the book INSIDE SS? If they are rather indefinite how were the drawings made so definitely.

Gosh, I wish I were over there, for I would like to see the casts.

Have a merry Christmas and be sure to keep it in your pants.

Cordially,

Gray Barker

In penultimate paragraph of letter above dated 8 December 1956 from "Kor" to Gray Barker, the *Mystic* magazine writer explains that only "some of the markings" are plainly visible from Orthon's footprints, versus Williamson's drawings of them in Adamski's books that depicted more distinct lines throughout. Follow-up letter from Barker to Kor dated 12 December 1956, also displayed here, asks for clarification on this matter. Venus author Cosmic Ray Keller and Northeast Ohio ufologist Michael LaRiche interview Kor at his home in the Greater Cleveland area in June 2018 and confirm Orthon's footprints were a small woman's moccasin or shoe, size six, and that the markings were too indistinct to arrive at any comprehensive conclusions. The real name of the alias "Peter Kor" has been blocked out of both letters to protect his identity.

***

Origins of the Richard Shaver Mystery

Perhaps the most phenomenal of paranormal experiencers was Richard Shaver. Like Peter Kor, Shaver was intimately associated with Raymond A. Palmer and all of his esoteric publications emanating out of Amherst, Wisconsin. Competition among science magazines, both factional and fictional, was tight throughout the 1940s. Palmer needed an edge, and he found it in the early 1943, when he presented his associate editor at *Amazing Stories*, Howard Browne, with a letter that had arrived in the mail from Dick Shaver of Berwick, Pennsylvania, purporting to reveal the truth about a race of malicious beings called the Dero that were living under the surface of the Earth. Palmer had read the long letter from beginning to end and then asked Browne for his opinion about it. "I read a third of it," said the associate editor, "and then I tossed it in the waste basket."

Palmer fished the document out of the "circular file," however, and kept it for future reference. He saw some great potential in Shaver as an up-and-coming science fiction writer. He polished up Shaver's article and then ran it in its entirety in the March 1945 issue of *Amazing Stories*. Palmer was delighted. A flood of mail came in. Readers of Amazing Stories insisted the story was true because they had been plagued by Deros or Dero-like creatures for years. The result was spectacular with sales of *Amazing Stories* shooting up through the roof. Subscriptions were up four-fold.

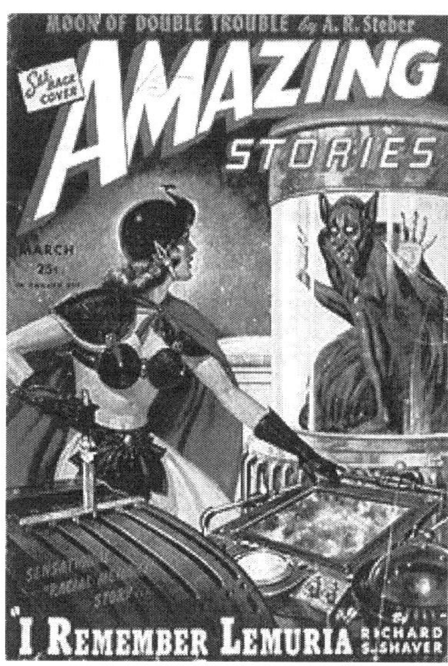

Richard Shaver's first novel, "I Remember Lemuria," appeared in the March 1945 issue of Raymond A. Palmer's Amazing Stories.

The Great Anomalist, John A. Keel, Pontificates

John A. Keel (1930-2009), the editor and publisher of *Anomaly*, and the author of numerous books and countless articles on flying saucers and other ongoing mysteries, was considered one of the greatest paranormal researchers of the twentieth century. In my opinion, one of Keel's most important articles, "The Man Who Invented Flying Saucers," appeared in the Winter1983, issue 41, of the *Fortean Times* (London, United Kingdom: Dennis Publishing). In an excellent biography of Raymond A. Palmer, Keel dedicates numerous paragraphs to Richard Shaver. Of particular bearing on the subject of this essay, Keel wrote the following concerning Shaver's account of the Dero and the rising popularity of *Amazing Stories:*

the Professional Cranks' Newsletter

ANOMALY

Published irregularly by:
Specialized Research
Box 351, Murray Hill Sta.
New York, N.Y. 10016

Not sold by subscription.
Send a stamped (20¢)self-addressed manila envelope for the next issue. Do not use air mail stamps. Include your zip code.

Vol.II-No. 1-Issue #11

APRIL 1974

John A. Keel edited the Anomaly newsletter, wrote countless articles and numerous books about our mysterious universe that he referred to as the "Super Spectrum."

***

Doing her part to raise feminist consciousness, Evelyn Smith of Indianapolis, Indiana, a.k.a. Captain Aura Rhanes, the Commander of the Spartacus, a Venusian observation patrol craft deployed from the far side of our Moon, posed for artist Ed Emshwiller of the Magazine of Fantasy and Science Fiction, October 1953 issue (Volume 5, Number 4), to highlight Kay Roger's story, "Letter to a Tiger," about a powerful female revolutionary from outer space. The heroine can pass through inter-dimensional gates. In a few months after this portrait appeared on the cover of the science fiction magazine, Captain Rhanes would visit radio engineer Dominick Lucchesi near his New Jersey home. See http://www.isfdb.org/cgi-bin/pl.cgi?61375.

"Actually, Palmer had accidentally tapped a huge, previously unrecognized audience. Nearly every community has at least one person who complains constantly to the local police that someone- usually a neighbor- is aiming a terrible ray gun at their house or apartment. This ray, they claim, is ruining their health, causing their plants to die, turning their bread moldy, making their hair and teeth fall out, and broadcasting voices in their heads.

"Psychiatrists are very familiar with these 'ray' victims and relate the problem with paranoid-schizophrenia. For the most part, these paranoiacs are harmless and usually elderly. Occasionally, however, the voices they hear urge them to perform destructive acts, particularly arson. They are a distrustful lot, loners by nature, and very suspicious of everyone, including the government and all figures of authority. In earlier times, they thought they were hearing the voice of God and/or the Devil.

"Today they often blame the Central Intelligence Agency (CIA) or space beings for their woes. They naturally gravitate to eccentric causes and organizations which reflect their own fears and insecurities, advocating bizarre political philosophies and reinforcing their peculiar belief systems. Ray Palmer unintentionally gave thousands of these people focus to their lives.

"Shaver's long, rambling letter claimed that while he was welding he heard voices which explained to him how the underground Deros were controlling life on the surface of the Earth through the use of fiendish rays."

In the footnotes to this article, Keel points out that, "It is interesting that so many victims of this type of phenomenon were welding or operating electrical equipment such as radios, radar, etc., when they began to hear voices."

For Dominick Lucchesi, this was the signal point for the entry of the Venusian observation patrol craft *Spartacus'* Captain Aura Rhanes.

***

You must understand though the touch of your hand, makes my pulse react.
That it's only the thrill of boy meeting girl, opposites attract. It's physical—only logical.
You must try to ignore that it means more than that. Ooooh! What's love got to do, got to do with it? What's love?—but a second hand emotion. What's love got to do—got to do with it?
Who needs a heart when a heart can be broken?

—Tina Turner, "What's Love Got to Do with It" in *Private Dancer* album, 1984
See http://www.kaltblut-magazine.com/tbt-tina-turner-whats-love-got-to-do-with-it/.

Chapter 7: Early Activities of the North Jersey U.F.O. Group

This chapter is dedicated to the New Jersey UFO research pioneers Frank Chille, Pat Marcattilio, a.k.a. "Dr. UFO," and Major George Filer, USAF, Ret., all continuing in the proud tradition of Lee Munsick and the North Jersey U.F.O. Group.

Getting Organized

New Jersey was at the epicenter of UFO activity on the East Coast of the United States from 1954-1965. In the Spring of 1954, some of the citizens of northern New Jersey concerned about the appearance of flying saucers in their skies organized themselves into the North Jersey U.F.O. Group, headquartered in Morristown and under the directorship of Lee R. Munsick, an advertising salesman at radio station WCRV, broadcasting out of Washington, New Jersey. Munsick resided on Beechwwod Drive in Morristown and had been following the flying saucer craze ever since he was a young teenager and civilian pilot Kenneth Arnold first reported nine disc-shaped objects zooming over the peaks of the Cascade Mountains in Washington State back on 24 June 1947. Most of the interested persons joining the new club already formed strong opinions about the U.F.O. phenomenon.

Those religiously inclined opined that the flying saucers were carrying angels on missionary journeys to save the lost souls of sinful but repenting Earthlings. Others, like director Munsick, were more apt to surmise that UFOs were manned spaceships visiting our world from some nearby planet in our own solar system, perhaps Mars or Venus. Munsick could only guess at the extraterrestrials' motives in coming here. All of the burgeoning New Jersey ufologists were quietly trying to learn the "who, what, when, where and why" of the strange objects being reported over their state by a plentitude of reliable witnesses. The members of the North Jersey U.F.O. Group have traveled up and down their state, interviewing anyone willing to talk about their UFO sighting.

In June of 1955, Munsick was in his early 20s. In an interview with Richard O. Shafer, a reporter from the local Morristown newspaper, Munsick admitted that he had an obsession about flying saucers, perhaps spending an inordinate amount of time researching the subject. Of the UFO enigma, he declared that, "I am one of those who think so-called flying saucers originated out of this world. As to where they come from, I don't know. They could be using the Moon as a base from which to observe the Earth." He qualified this statement by adding that, "If they're real and occupied by beings, it is well worth knowing who they are and what they're doing. Maybe we'll never find out until they come down and bomb us or prove friendly."

The huge increase in UFO sightings across the world in 1954 spurred Munsick's curiosity about the phenomenon, providing the impetus for a more active engagement with the subject. He put an advertisement in the newspaper asking other New Jersey residents with an interest in flying saucers to get in touch with him through Morristown Post Office Box 606. About thirty individuals responded and the North Jersey U.F.O. Group was born. The membership pooled their UFO books into a sharing library and circulated a list of books that local residents could check out from their group to inform themselves about the true nature of the UFO phenomenon. A special committee prepared a questionnaire that director Munsick could send to anyone who claimed to have seen a UFO or encountered its occupant(s).

The director lamented that, "Some flying saucer groups are composed of crackpots and swindlers" just trying to make a buck off all of the interest out there in UFOs. The need for a serious organization like the North Jersey U.F.O. Group had been apparent; and that is why Munsick took the bold step in assembling it. The group has also been exchanging information with other groups from around the United States and the world. The leadership of the North Jersey U.F.O. Group also played an integral role in helping to launch the National Investigations Committee on Aerial Phenomena in Washington, D.C. (NICAP).

A Dream Realized

Following the demise of Albert K. Bender's International Flying Saucer Bureau, which endured from 1952-1953, the field of ufology in the United States was in complete disarray with a smattering of local groups trying to pick up the pieces, and the slack. Yes, these disparate UFO groups were cooperating as they could, on a limited basis, but they all had their own agendas with respect to the phenomenon; and their primary concerns rested with respective membership bases. For Lee Munsick, this situation was untenable.

In late September and early October of 1956, Munsick made a hurried trip to the nation's capital to speak about the dire state of American ufology with the Washington UFO Discussion Group. At the meeting, Munsick stressed the need for a national flying saucer organization. He also made time to speak privately with Clara John, the editor and publisher of the prestigious *Little Listening Post*. John's bimonthly newsletter was put together out of her home at 4811 Illinois Avenue, N.W., in Washington, D.C., and went out to several thousand subscribers, all active participants in their local UFO clubs. The subscribers carried on a long and intimate correspondence with John and the activities of their local organizations were featured prominently in the pages of the *Little Listening Post*. The subscribers also forwarded newspaper clippings about UFO sightings and encounters from their particular areas; and John saw to it that the more prominent reports found their way into the pages of her periodical.

Munsick also met with the renowned UFO author Morris K. Jessup, who also lived in the environs of Washington D.C. Munsick was duly impressed with Jessup's array of flying saucer books, published by Citadel in New York City: *Case for the UFO* (1955), the *1955 UFO Annual* (1956), and the *Expanding Case for the UFO*, which he just finished and was scheduled to arrive in bookstores nationwide in January of the following year. Munsick maintained a ufology bookstore and library for the membership of the North Jersey U.F.O. Group and ensured that UFO books could be checked out without charge for all members of the North Jersey U.F.O. Group and that all current UFO books were in stock and could be purchased at cost.

Of Jessup and his major work, *Case for the UFO*, Munsick informed the New Jersey membership that the UFO author was both an "explorer and instructor at the University of Michigan who gives a complete story on UFOs and a summary of the situation as it is today. Astronomical reports of mysterious objects, lights and fireballs, meteorological phenomena, things falling from the sky, and UFOs as recorded back in history.... Mr. Jessup brings together a lot of facts, and catalogues them to give detailed accounts to read."

In his Washington D.C. meeting with Jessup, Munsick also learned that Jessup was working on yet another, but extremely controversial book, tentatively titled the *Bible Case for the UFO*. This book would be based on the *Pentateuch*, or the five books of Moses at the beginning of the *Old Testament*. Remember, this was twelve years before Erich von Däniken came out with his *Chariots of the Gods* (New York: G. P. Putnam's Sons, 1968). Munsick respected Jessup's courage in trying to publish the *Bible Case for the UFO*, at least insofar as it ran up against the religious establishment of the day in advocating a materialist concept of creation, the evolution of intelligent life and our unfolding scientific knowledge of the universe.

In the *UFO Annual*, Jessup also ran afoul of the powers-that-be. In that fully illustrated tome, apart from a chronological listing of saucer sightings and details for 1955, the Michigan professor included the vital and complete text of Air Force Regulation 200-2, revised to 12 August 1954. This classified document includes the ruling that set up the federal UFO reporting system, security measures and penalties involved for any breaches thereof. Munsick encouraged all of the New Jersey group's membership to buy the book, insofar as it was "heartily recommended" by him. However, this was 1956 in the heart of an America racked by McCarthyism and in the grips of the Cold War. Jessup once again proved himself a brave soul, indeed, as did Munsick for sticking by him.

In my considered opinion, this was one of the least recognized but important missions undertaken by an individual researcher in the history of private UFO investigative organizations. For after much talk and prolonged hoping, a national flying saucer organization was finally born. Within days of the conclusion of the meeting of the Washington UFO Discussion Group, NICAP was incorporated in the District of Columbia as a non-profit organization. This meant that even the membership fees paid were tax deductible. At its head was T. Townsend Brown, a respected physicist well known for his research on gravity.

When Munsick returned to Morristown, New Jersey, he proudly informed his group that, "NICAP's prospectus indicates a vast field of endowed work which should be of tremendous help, not only to civilian research organizations such as ours but to various government agencies and other research groups. Their program appears to require between one quarter and half a million dollars. Office space has been taken in Washington. NICAP is asking for individual memberships ($15.00) and for books. If you have spare books, send them to PROJECT SKYLIGHT, 1536 Connecticut Avenue, N.W., Washington 6, D.C. Write your name and address on the flyleaf as donator."

The Balloon Goes Up

On Saturday, 13 October 1956, most of northern New Jersey was in turmoil as a spectacular sphere was brilliantly reflected against a clear Indian summer sky. The object was distinctly seen by thousands. On the following day, New Jersey newspapers reported that most people had seen nothing more than a weather balloon launched by the Weather Bureau at Idlewild International Airport at 4:30 p.m. A spokesman for the Weather Bureau informed the reporters that these types of balloons are launched all the time, but that unusual atmospheric conditions made this particular balloon to appear like a spherical UFO. The spokesman said that all weather balloons lifting off from Idewild carry radio transmitters which pass on information like temperature, humidity, etc., and are tracked on radar to determine their direction and wind speed. The ascension rate for such a balloon is 1,000 feet per minute. Such a balloon can reach an altitude of 54,000 feet and remain aloft for about one and a half hours. The Weather Bureau spokesman noted that because of this flight data, "We may assume the balloon could be seen between eastern Pennsylvania and Long Island between 4:30 and 6:00 p.m."

Lee Munsick's residential telephone, which also served as the primary communications for reporting sightings to the North Jersey U.F.O. Group, was ringing off the hook from early Saturday afternoon all the way through Tuesday evening. Everyone was questioning the press reports. Their personal observations did not jive with the explanations put forth in the newspapers. They just didn't make any sense. For example, another object and multiple objects were sighted over Wilkes-Barre, Pennsylvania, around 2 p.m. on Saturday. This was two and a half hours before the balloon was sent up at Idlewild and beyond any projected flight path for it.

Munsick checked into this situation and did discover that another balloon was launched by the Weather Bureau at Idlewild at 10:30 a.m. that day; but it should have descended by noon. Another spherical object was seen at Mt. Lakes, New Jersey from 4 p.m. to as late as 8:00 p.m. Munsick personally checked back with the Weather Bureau and was told that, "Early information indicated some sightings might be caused by the Constant Pressure Research Project at Princeton University which used to launch plastic balloons." However, the intrepid Munsick discovered that the project was not currently operational in the area, but had been transferred to the College of Pennsylvania and the General Mills project in Kalamazoo, Michigan.

Thanks to the foundational research accomplished by the North Jersey U.F.O. Group in the 1950s and 1960s, contemporary UFO investigations continue at a steady clip in the Garden State. See https://www.buzzfeed.com/danmeth/11-hours-at-a-ufo-conference-in-new-jersey?utm_term=.nnERPbPjn#.hjnxGaGpB.

Seeking Structure

On 13 September 1955, at 8:30 p.m., Lee Munsick and eight other New Jersey residents that had been irregularly meeting in each others' homes to discuss various aspects of the flying saucer phenomenon, assembled in the residence of William Earl Tucker at 11 Moore Terrace in West Orange, New Jersey, for the purpose of officially establishing the North Jersey U.F.O. Group. Lee Munsick had been serving as the group's provisional director since they first started to get together in the spring of 1954; hence he was presiding. Others in attendance were Fred Bierwirth of Bergenfield, Mr. and Mrs. Stanley Crane of Maywood, Edward W. Kesgen of East Rutherford, Harold S. Tauer of Paterson, Ted Collen of Whippany and William Wilson of Morristown.

The meeting began with a general discussion. Wilson discussed the progress of the work being accomplished by UFO discussion groups in Kearfott and Morristown. He praised Munsick's efforts in working with a local bookstore to make current UFO books and periodicals available to the community. Wilson noted that the group's own periodical file had been updated and correspondence was initiated with the leadership of other UFO groups from the United States and around the world. Collen said that he heard about the UFO group through the local bookstore and was already meeting with a small group of interested persons out in Kearfott. Collen expressed concern about the proliferation of the fanatic fringe and phony religions in ufology. These were hindering the important work of reaching the masses with an objective truth about UFOs. Collen was working to keep the more radical elements separate from the Kearfott and Morristown groups. He hoped these two smaller groups would become a larger scientific and unitary organization.

UFO Sightings

Earl Tucker built a deck in his backyard to serve as a UFO observation post. He explained about a verified sighting of a flying saucer he had from this post and invited other members of the North Jersey U.F.O. Group to call ahead and come visit his house for UFO sky watch parties. Like the contactee George Adamski on the slopes of Mt. Palomar in California, Tucker set up a small reflecting telescope for the benefit of any visitors. Tucker encouraged members visiting his home to bring their cameras in the hope of taking a UFO photograph.

Stanley Crane and his wife just returned from a visit to Mexico City where they met with a George Adamski flying saucer contact group. The New Jersey couple joined hands with the Adamski followers in a circle and transmitted their thoughts to the Venusians in orbit to send down a scout ship. None of the assembled believers were disappointed; as a flying saucer dropped down out of a cloud bank and over the city's skyline; whence it hovered for about 30 seconds before it sped quickly out of sight, zipping off in a southeasterly direction, toward the Popocatépetl volcano. The director of the Mexico City contact group, a local cab driver Salvador Villanueva Medina, said he had an encounter with some Venusians after his taxi broke down on the outskirts of Ciudad Vallejo in mid-August 1953. Adamski made a special trip to Mexico City just for the purpose of meeting with Villanueva in March 1955. The details of their meeting were relayed in chapter nine of Bryant and Helen Reeves, *Flying Saucer Pilgrimage* (Amherst, Wisconsin: Amherst Press, 1957). The book was listed as an "inspired novel," but of course, it was certainly much more than that.

Photograph taken by Bryant Reeve in March 1955 in Mexico City, depicts Polish-American contactee George Adamski (L) with Mexican contactee Salvador Villanueva Medina (R), who share accounts of their close encounters with Venusians and other extraterrestrials visiting Earth.

Statement of Policy

Lee Munsick had developed the Statement of Policy for the North Jersey U.F.O. Group on 1 September 1955, which was unanimously approved by all in attendance at the 13 September 1955 historic meeting. This is a very important document in the annals of ufology insofar as it established general guidelines for the evolution of one of the earliest UFO investigations groups.

According to the statement, the purpose of the North Jersey U.F.O. Group was:

1. To consolidate the efforts of various interested persons inquiring into the mystery of the flying saucer phenomenon. To establish the identity of, or determine the specific purpose of these phenomena.
2. To collect detailed information, maintain a central file on all confidential reports, published material and correspondence. To issue a report form on receipt of notice of any sighting or contact with flying saucers.
3. To act as a source of information for, and offer services to, all press, radio and TV facilities, as well as local libraries. Available on instant notice to all enforcement and investigative agencies, to assist in evaluation at time of contact.
4. To offer a unified, but informal procedure for meetings of the group whenever deemed necessary. To obtain qualified speakers for such, and promote a program to insure members being well-informed. To establish liaison with other groups in the field.
5. To sponsor a program to bring the subject before the public, thereby increasing the size and usefulness of the group.

In conformity with the agenda carried out in the 13 September meeting, a press release was drawn up by Lee Munsick and released on 29 September 1955 announcing the formation of the North Jersey U.F.O. Group to the world at large. Munsick stressed that, "Our group is completely serious in this matter. We feel it is not a humorous situation, but one into which work and research must go before anyone is qualified to interpret the available information."

Conflicts with the Government

Project Bluebook, headquartered at Wright-Patterson Air Force Base in Dayton, Ohio, had officially been empowered to investigate UFO reports since its establishment in 1948. On Tuesday, 25 October 1955, Air Force Secretary Donald A. Quarles issued a confusing statement about the UFO phenomenon. The secretary noted that many UFO sightings could probably be explained as the misidentification of conventional or even experimental aircraft, that only a very small percentage of UFO reports could not be explained, and that most likely Project Bluebook would continue to be funded, albeit on an interim basis.

Quarles and others in the Air Force hierarchy were well aware that interest in UFOs was on the upswing nationally. Americans were organizing themselves into UFO clubs across the country. The growing membership in these groups appeared to be developing into a national movement, as would later prove to be the case with the emergence of the powerful NICAP. If the Air Force could keep local groups from forming, the brass would sleep safely in knowing that they maintained an intellectual hegemony over any scientific interpretations offered to explain the UFO enigma.

On 27 October 1955, Musick issued a press statement declaring that, "The North Jersey U.F.O. Group intends to pursue its planned studies in the field of 'flying saucers.'" In addressing recent technological developments in the aerospace industry, he added that, "We have known for some time that work in this field was being done at Avro, Ltd., in Canada, and at Ryan Aeronautical Company in California. It should be noticed that the new saucer-shaped craft is jet-powered. But most of the sightings we have investigated, and the information with which we work, do not include jet- or even rocket-propelled bodies. We had hoped that the government would be successful in its work with electro-magnetic or anti-gravity propulsion, but it appears that this is not the case."

Prototype of the Avro Aerocar, produced in Canada for the U.S. Air Force, only goes to show that contactee Gabriel Green was correct when he said that, "UFOs are real. The Air Force is an illusion."

It was evident to Munsick and others in the membership of the North Jersey U.F.O. Group that the UFOs were evidencing a technology far surpassing anything extant in the United States of the year 1955. However, Munsick did note that, "The immediate effect of the Air Force release at this time is that our work will be harder in the future, with American saucers in the air." He added that, "Our screenings of sightings will be more difficult than before; but I feel our work, though altered, will continue. It is interesting to note that the Air Force statement comes on the heels of recent statements by a cabinet-rank British official that saucers are real but not of Earthly origin. Also, publicity is due presently, regarding a new book by Major Donald Keyhoe, USMC, Ret., who has in the past worked with the Air Force on the subject; and a lecture series by Desmond Leslie, British pilot and author. Another author lecturing in the United States at this time is Mr. M. K. Jessup, who wrote *A Case for the UFO*. He is giving a talk before an associated group in New York, on Friday night."

The associated group Munsick was referring to was the Civilian Saucer Intelligence (CSI) in New York City. Working closely with Munsick and the North Jersey U.F.O. Group, the CSI leadership was also counted among the prime instigators for the foundation of NICAP. Desmond Leslie, of royal peerage, it should be added, was the co-author with California contactee George Adamski of the wildly successful *Flying Saucers Have Landed* (London, United Kingdom: British Book Centre, 1953).

In further addressing Quarles' press release, Munsick went on to say that, "This material continues in a series of confusing statements from the Air Force, issued over a period of several years. This is apparently part of an urgent program designed to quiet the growing interest in the subject. This series has been as contradictive as it has been uneven in timing. To illustrate, the report from a wire service quoted a spokesman as saying that *Project Bluebook*, the Air Force saucer investigating agency, would be continued. But is there any need for this action now, when the Air Force says there is nothing to investigate? Is this not a waste of the taxpayers' money?" Munsick goes even further, declaring, "But the contradiction goes further, for the last word on *Project Bluebook* was that it had been abandoned and closed down completely. We have known, however, that this was not the case. This is another attempt to stifle the tremendous interest in UFOs. Our mail has been so heavy in the past month that we cannot keep up with it. And we cover only northern New Jersey."

Then Munsick turned his attention to the UFO sightings being investigated by the Air Force *Project Bluebook*. "As to the three percent unexplained sightings, but considering the large number of sightings appearing, larger than the Air Force admits, even three percent is quite a few." Realizing that he was stepping on the Air Force's proverbial toes, Munsick continued to elaborate the stand of his organization by stating that, "The North Jersey U.F.O. Group intends to pursue its activity in the field in an unprejudiced manner. We hope that the Air Force will cooperate, along with other government agencies, more than in the past. And we still want very much to hear from anyone knowing of any information about 'flying saucers.'"

The Group and Alliance Strengthened

At the next meeting of the North Jersey U.F.O. Group, held on 10 November 1955, at 9 p.m., in the Paterson YMCA at 128 Ward Street, there were 18 in attendance. Munsick was chairman and explained the balloting procedures. The provisional three-person Central Committee was going to be expanded to a standing committee of five by appointment from the chair; and this resolution was approved by a vote of seven to one. This would be accomplished by 1 January 1956. A design for membership cards was also approved; and membership fees for the coming year of 1956 were set at two dollars. A resolution was also enacted to establish admission fees for future meetings, although an exact amount had not been set. All of these resolutions passed unanimously, eight to zero. Ted Collen was also appointed, by a vote of six to one with Collen abstaining, to head up the Technical Research Committee. It was also determined that field agents would be needed for the seven districts in the area of jurisdiction set apart for the North Jersey U.F.O. Group, and that a secretary would be needed to take stenographic notes of the meetings. It was hoped that all of these positions could be filled as the group's dues-paying membership base expanded.

A delegation attended from the CSI in New York City, with whom the Central Committee of the New Jersey group had been working quite closely. The delegates from New York took an active part in the general discussion period, which was most helpful. A press release specifying the ongoing cooperation between the two groups in saucer investigations was to be released on 17 November 1955 in both New Jersey and New York states. Several phases of joint activities and investigations were discussed. The joint leadership envisioned the formation of a national civilian saucers investigative group in the nation's capital, especially as linkages were being formed with yet more local clubs and organizations throughout the country.

Slide from Dr. Raymond A. Keller's Venus Rising presentation, "The Contactees," shown at bookstores, libraries and flying saucer club meetings throughout the United States.

Gray Barker Comes to Morristown

In 1956, the North Jersey U.F.O. Group had emerged as the second most influential and powerful saucer investigations organization in the East Coast region. Overall, the leadership's alliance with New York's Civilian Saucer Intelligence (CSI) was pushing the group more in the direction of so-called "scientific research" into the various aspects of the UFO phenomenon. The CSI, on the other hand, was in the process of developing a more restrictive policy in its acceptance of UFO reports deemed worthy of investigation. Most of the contact cases were being eschewed, automatically being written off as hoaxes, or of dubious credibility, at best. Unfortunately, this narrow attitude would carry over into the establishment of Washington, D.C.'s National Investigations Committee on Aerial Phenomena (NICAP). The CSI leadership little realized that the rise of NICAP would herald the end of their organization. Ultimately, it was to become absorbed into NICAP, becoming just one of their many chapters in the state of New York.

Lee Munsick astutely saw the need to maintain the independence of the North Jersey U.F.O. Group. Working with the CSI and NICAP would be beneficial; but Munsick was not about the throw out investigations into the area of possible extraterrestrial contacts with human beings. Munsick surmised that if aliens from other planets were traversing the vast distances of outer space to get to the Earth, they would certainly get out of their flying saucers to communicate with the local inhabitants. After all, if we sent a spaceship to Venus and found out it was inhabited, wouldn't we want to contact at least a few of the Venusians to find out as much about their biology, culture, language, etc.? In consideration of this question, Munsick took it upon himself to invite various speakers associated with the extraterrestrial contact movement; and the preeminent spokesperson for this esoteric subject, at the time, was none other than Gray Barker of Clarksburg, West Virginia.

Significance of the Barker Meeting

A press release was issued by Munsick on behalf of the group to local papers throughout northern New Jersey about a week before the event, announcing the appearance of Gray Barker at the Thursday, 24 May 1956 meeting. Expecting a large crowd, the venue was set as the Griffith Foundation Auditorium at 605 Broad Street in Newark. The meeting would start promptly at 8:15 p.m. Admission for members was set at fifty cents and one dollar for non-members.

This would be one of the more important appearances of Gray Barker in his long career in ufology. Barker had declared that, "Certain researchers and investigators found out where the flying saucers come from, but were forced to keep the information secret." Barker just completed his work on a new book, *They Knew Too Much About Flying Saucers* (New York: University Books, 1956), which was released to the public for the first time at the Newark meeting.

At the meeting, Barker talked about his controversial book. He related how one UFO investigator, Albert K. Bender, director of the International Flying Saucer Bureau (1952-1953), was visited by three mysterious strangers in black suits and told to "shut up" about flying saucers. "Other investigators have also been frightened into silence," Barker warned those in attendance who might have been considering a career in UFO investigations.

There were slightly over 300 in attendance; so Munsick and the Central Committee of the North Jersey U.F.O. Group were happy. The auditorium was full. Barker told those assembled that he first became interested in flying saucer reports when he investigated the so-called "Flatwoods Monster," which allegedly landed in a spaceship and terrorized seven witnesses on a dark hillside in Braxton County, West Virginia, back in 1952. The sighting of this space creature made headlines around the world. Barker was convinced that the stories provided by the witnesses were true and he launched a three-year investigation into the incident. Barker started up one of the first UFO publications, *The Saucerian*, back in 1953, to write about the Flatwoods Monster and other sightings of UFOs and attendant creatures coming to his attention from dozens of countries. Back in 1956, there were already some 25 monthly publications like *The Saucerian* focusing exclusively on the UFO enigma.

Having been the head of the English Department in a Maryland public school system, Barker proved to be an excellent chronicler and writer about UFO events. He also worked as an audio-visual education consultant for a large school supplier and the manager of one of the nation's first drive-in movie theaters, specializing in science fiction films, of course. Barker noted that his interest in the Flatwoods case sparked his enthusiasm for flying saucer research as a hobby, but that with the ever-increasing amount of time spent on investigating UFO cases, he quickly realized the "stark reality behind the mystery."

Barker Meets a Local Contactee

The historic 24 May 1956 meeting proved quite fortuitous for Gray Barker. Howard Menger of High Bridge, New Jersey, was one of the newer members of the North Jersey U.F.O. Group who was in attendance that evening. Menger had previously discussed his encounters with Venusians and other extraterrestrials that had been landing their flying saucers in an apple orchard in the backyard of his High Bridge farmhouse with Lee Munsick and other members of the North Jersey U.F.O. Group. Munsick wasn't quite sure what to make out of Menger's claims.

Menger insisted that his first encounter with a Venusian took place when he was just ten years old, back in 1932. He and his little brother Alan were playing in the backyard when they saw a flying saucer swoop down over the apple orchard. There was a flash of light near a large rock that immediately attracted their attention, whence a beautiful woman materialized, sitting upon the rock. The woman explained that she was over 500 years old and from the planet Venus. She explained to Howard that he had an important mission of peace to carry out on behalf of the brothers and sisters of other planets and that the Venusians and other extraterrestrials would be assisting him throughout the remainder of his incarnation on the physical Earth plane of existence.

Gray Barker, pioneer ufologist (1925-1984): Photo courtesy of Harrison County Public Library, Clarksburg, West Virginia.

Insofar as Menger was writing a book about his encounters and Gray Barker was the publisher of a UFO magazine as well as the author of a greatly anticipated UFO book, Munsick thought it would be good to introduce these two enigmatic personalities to each other. After the meeting, Barker, at Munsick's behest, took the time to meet with Menger. Barker wasn't sure if Menger's experience was imagined or real, but he sensed that Menger believed it. For Barker, his first impression of Menger's story was that it definitely had the potential of being a best-seller, rivaling in sales receipts the books of the California contactee, George Adamski. Barker agreed to edit Menger's book when he finished writing it and to publish it through his own Saucerian Press.

The book was titled *From Outer Space to You* (Clarksburg, West Virginia: Saucerian Press, 1959), and truly emerged the success that Barker envisioned it would be. Menger was a sign painter and not a journalist or professional writer. I have examined the entire original text, and noted that Gray Barker had to do a lot of editing on the manuscript to get the book to flow as nicely as it does. I provided a summary of Menger's encounters in the first book in my Venus trilogy, *Venus Rising: A Concise History of the Second Planet* (Terra Alta, West Virginia: Headline Books, 2015), for your convenience. The book is available on amazon.com, while supplies last. The painting at the beginning of this article was commissioned by Barker for inclusion in the first edition of Menger's book.

A Discrepancy Noted

In working with the archives o f the North Jersey U.F.O. Group, however, I discovered a discrepancy in the way that Howard Menger presented his first encounter with the beautiful Venusian woman to UFO groups before his book was published by Barker's Saucerian Press, versus the manner it was framed afterwards. In private correspondence from Munsick to Barker, dated 13 January 1959, Munsick writes in his third paragraph:

> "Now, the next matter revolves about our mutual friend, Howard Menger, 'Writer, lecturer, radio and TV personality….' it says here. Really, Gray! I notice a chapter title, 'The Girl on the Rock.' I wonder if this tale is the first one he told us, or the one altered for public use. You know originally she was entirely nude, then for radio use, he provided her with some demure clothing! Actually I find more to laugh about Howard than anything else, mainly because I got to know him really well, and found him perfectly charming. But his story."

Barker seems to have been stunned by this blockbuster information that Munsick laid on him; for he doesn't write back to the chair of the North Jersey U.F.O. Group until 23 February 1959, where he states in his fourth paragraph that:

> "I hadn't heard that the Girl on the Rock was originally in the nude. Perhaps that was the real story that Howard knew he would have to tone down for lectures and publication. As to whether or not I believe Menger, let me say I am merely publishing his book, with the idea that it is up to the reader whether or not to accept it as truth or how much of it to accept as truth. As soon as the book is out, I'll see that you get a free review copy.
>
> "I don't handle any of Menger's photos—am just publishing the book. I'm sure that in that you know Menger well you would only have to ask him to get what photos you need."

Venusians lack the Earthlings' unwarranted inhibitions about the human body. Howard Menger had to proceed with caution in explaining his first encounter with the "Girl on the Rock."

In my three-part series, "The Kenneth Arnold Files," published originally on Lon Strickler's blog site, www.phantomsandmonsters.com/2017/11/the-kenneth-arnold-files-part-i, www.phantomsandmonsters.com/2017/12/the-kenneth-arnold-files-part-ii, and www.phantomsandmonsters.com/2018/01/the-kenneth-arnold-files-part-iii, I wrote of several cases where Venusians appeared in the buff and discussed the Venusian approach to nudism unencumbered by Earthly strictures of morality. The discovery of the North Jersey U.F.O. Group correspondence between its director Munsick and the prolific Saucerian writer Gray Barker serve to validate the contentions made in my Kenneth Arnold investigations and series.

Chapter 8: Dr. James E. McDonald and the Extraterrestrial Hypothesis

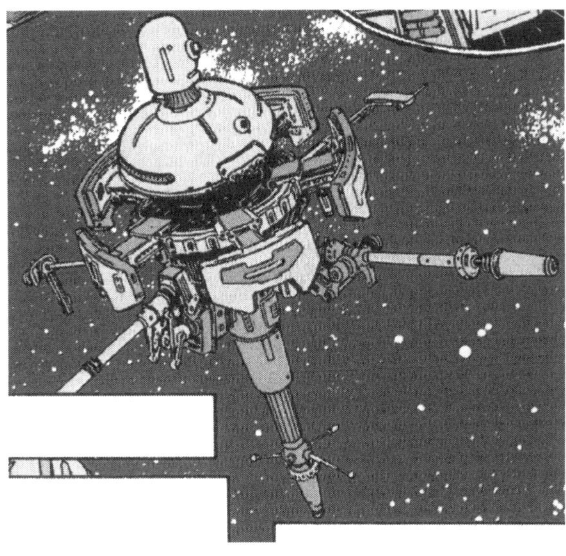

In the Star Wars movies, spacecraft employing hyper-drive technology made use of this "lighthouse network" of fixed-position beacons. These devices recorded local hyperspace data, which was then downloaded by visiting spacecraft. Apparently, every beacon served as a massive supercomputer in space that kept accurate data on hyperspace routes that could be accessed by spacecraft seeking to make hyperspace jumps within limited distances and direction in the local galactic sector. For example, a local network might require as many as twenty jump beacons. An individual spaceship would also transmit astronomical navigation information to the rest of the network when passing through hyperspace. Was George Lucas inspired by the speculations of the late physicist and pioneer UFO researcher, Dr. James E. McDonald? See http://starwars.wikia.com/wiki/Hyperspace_beacon.

Some of the prominent space scientists of the 1960s were starting to lean strongly in favor of the extraterrestrial hypothesis. Dr. James E. McDonald (1920-1971) was one of these. Dr. McDonald suggested that some UFOs might best be explained as actual, physical spacecraft occupied by advanced extraterrestrial life or non-human aliens from other planets visiting our world, despite being remotely tucked away, as it is, on the rim of the Milky Way galaxy. Dr. McDonald was a noted American physicist and tenured professor in the Department of Meteorology, University of Arizona at Tucson. He was best known for his research into the UFO phenomenon.

In an interview with Major H. C. Petersen, co-editor of Denmark's *UFO Contact*, published in the June 1968 edition, Dr. McDonald commented that, "It is remotely possible that newly detected, mysterious signals from outer space may be galactic navigational beacons being employed by an advanced civilization to guide their manned spaceships along the Milky Way."

When asked to elaborate on these signals, Dr. McDonald remarked that, "While radio astronomers making the observations are reluctant to speculate publicly on artificial origins, they are talking privately about the possibility that these sources are navigation beacons or segments of a communication net linking a number of highly advanced civilizations."

The physicist continued: "Given that intelligent beings may be traveling the immense voids of outer space, and assuming it is possible that certain regular pattern, 100-day interval signals have been received by radio astronomers here on Earth, even space travelers far ahead of our technology could lose their way in the bustling environs of interstellar space."

Dr. McDonald further speculated that, "Perhaps immensely powerful radio beacons, placed at strategic points in the starry void, are transmitting regular pattern signals. Even if they are not aimed directly at us, the signals might be produced by an intelligent civilization as directional beams or light houses for a space navigation system. We have already used similar systems for air and sea navigation. It is possible that some civilization could have set up a space navigation system based on these signals."

What was really remarkable about these statements from Dr. McDonald was that they were made in the late 1960s, when most scientists scoffed at the very notion that any kind of extraterrestrial life might exist, let alone be traveling the great expanse of the universe in flying saucers. Since the late 1940s, with UFOs appearing in greater numbers in our skies, most scientists had rejected out of hand the reported visitations to Earth of any extraterrestrial spacecraft and their crews.

Science and UFOs

Dr. McDonald firmly believed that some truisms could be established concerning science, technology and UFOs. In an address delivered to the employees and scientists attending the general seminar of the United Aircraft Research Laboratories of East Hartford, Connecticut, on 26 January 1968, Dr. McDonald declared that, "Proud as we can be of today's cumulative record of scientific exploration of the world about us, we certainly do not know all that deserves the name of fundamental scientific knowledge….," adding that, "A truism about technology that has strong bearing on what I shall be saying about UFOs today is this: Given time, an edifice of expanding technology far more impressive than that which we see about us in 1968 could be erected simply on the basis of the present stock of fundamental scientific knowledge."

By this, the doctor made reference to the magnitude of the technological edifice that would surely expand proportionately with the seemingly exponential increase of future scientific discoveries with respect to the UFO phenomenon. Our future understanding of the enigma would be unforeseeably and vastly greater than anything afforded by the then contemporary technology of the late 1960s. That here we are, fifty years later, and no closer to the truth may, in my humble opinion, be more a matter of the lack of disclosure by the military, political and scientific powers-that-be than any fault of discovery by investigating parties.

The astute physicist maintained that, "A truism about modern man's outlook on nature and on his place therein that has strong bearing on the present status of the UFO problem is this: In his centuries-long struggle out of slavery to superstition and fear of the supernatural, modern science-oriented man has developed subtle but well-ingrained dispositions to reject observations and reports of the anomalous and the inexplicable; and that rejection is the more vehement the farther the observations seem to lie beyond the pale of present-day science."

Another truism about UFOs that Dr. McDonald discussed at length in the general seminar was that since the great flying saucer flap of the summer of 1947, the majority of scientists had come to view UFOs as a "nonsense problem." For the most part, the subject of UFOs was deserving of nothing but scorn, or silent disdain. "Throughout the entire world," said Dr.

McDonald, "only a small handful of scientists have taken the trouble to attempt direct checks on the puzzling and recurring reports of UFO phenomena; compared with that handful, there has been a large and rather vocal group who have either explicitly or indirectly ridiculed the notion that there might be unconventional craft-like objects operating over our planet; and their scoffing has been based not upon extensive personal investigations of UFO reports but primarily upon *a priori* considerations."

Dr. James E. McDonald (1920-1971), American physicist; did he know too much about flying saucers?

Dr. J. Allen Hynek, an astronomer of Northwestern University and a technical consultant to the Air Force *Project Blue Book* at the time, would eventually come to agree wholeheartedly with fellow scientist McDonald's assessment about the typical skeptic's operating from an agenda formed from preconceived notions that automatically invalidated the scientific substance of any UFO investigations.

Most of the derision from the so-called scientific community of the late 1960s was directed against the purveyors of the extraterrestrial hypothesis (ETH). It is therefore understood that the ETH asserts that at least some UFOs are types of extraterrestrial probes or vehicles, the products of some technology other than our own, and decidedly more advanced.

Scientist as UFO Investigator

Throughout his life, Dr. McDonald personally interviewed over 500 UFO witnesses and many UFO experiencers. He also uncovered many important and classified documents concerning the UFO phenomenon from United States government archives. Dr. McDonald was noted as one of the more vocal opponents of the government-funded *Scientific Study of Unidentified Flying Objects* (1966-1968), led by Dr. Edward U. Condon of the University of Colorado at Boulder that recommended the closure of *Project Blue Book* and an end to further government sponsored UFO research. *Project Blue Book* was shut down in 1969, but UFO investigations continued to be clandestinely carried out by other United States government agencies up to our current day.

As we continue in this chapter, we discover how Dr. J. Allen Hynek was secretly working with Dr. James E. McDonald behind the scenes of American scientific academia to expose the United States government's cover-up of UFO secrets. We also explore the mysterious circumstances surrounding the alleged suicide of Dr. McDonald, just another scientist who knew too much about flying saucers.

Scene above from sci-fi classic movie, This Island Earth (Universal International Pictures, 1955): Before entering the stasis chamber preparatory to interstellar flight aboard a flying saucer from the embattled planet Metaluna, space scientist Dr. Ruth Adams (Faith Domergue) turns to her associate, electronics wizard Dr. Cal Meacham (Rex Reason), to inquire, "Tell me again, Cal, whose lame idea was it, in the first place, to research UFOs?"

***

In the closing years of the 1960s, scientific mindsets were slowly changing with respect to the UFO phenomenon. In the previous installment, we came to see how the extraterrestrial hypothesis became firmly embraced by Dr. James E. McDonald, a prominent American physicist and tenured professor in the Department of Meteorology at the University of Arizona at Tucson. The doctor took a long-range view of UFOs, declaring at the 26 January 1968 meeting of the United Aircraft Research Laboratories in East Hartford, Connecticut, that:

"After about eighteen months of study and direct interviewing of about three hundred witnesses in important UFO cases, I can say to you that I see the UFO problem as one of extraordinary scientific importance.

"I regard the extraterrestrial hypothesis (ETH) as the most probable hypothesis to explain the UFO evidence. To go from that expression of hypothesis-preference to a position of claiming adequate proof is no small step, needless to say. That step will not be taken until quite large financial resources are behind monitoring and observation programs, supported by budgets that will probably dwarf the NASA budgets. And that step will not be taken until large numbers of scientists in many disciplines begin to confront the enormously intriguing questions posed by the UFOs. If my remarks to you today serve in any small measure to increase the number of scientists and engineers seriously concerned with the UFO problem, I shall consider my time well spent."

Staying Clear of Cults

Dr. McDonald was aware of competing theories with the ETH. He found the following grouping of these theories to be quite useful in his scientific investigations:

1. Hoaxes, fabrications and frauds.
2. Hallucinations, mass hysteria and rumor phenomena.
3. Lay interpretation of well-known physical phenomena (meteorological, astronomical, optical, etc.).
4. Advanced technologies (test vehicles, satellites, re-entry phenomena, etc.).
5. Poorly understood physical phenomena (rare atmospheric-electrical effects, cloud phenomena, plasmas of natural or technological origin, etc.).
6. Poorly understood psychological phenomena, and lastly
7. Messengers of salvation and occult truth.

From year to year since the Air Force began officially investigating UFO reports in 1948 under the auspices of Project Sign, and subsequently under Projects Grudge and Bluebook, the batting average for explaining away most UFO phenomena was varying between 88 and 90%. But there were always at the end of each year a persistent number of cases truly remaining in the classification of "unidentified." These are the ones that Dr. McDonald considered as the best prospects for finding a true visiting spacecraft of extraterrestrial origin. For the most part, Dr. McDonald did not dispute that all of these categories offered viable explanations for the vast majority of UFO reports; but he was particularly miffed with category eight, messengers of salvation and occult truth, because in his estimation, as a scientist with a materialist philosophy of looking at the universe, anything smacking of the supernatural would only cloud and detract from the application of the ETH to the encounters and sightings falling into the unidentified slot. The physicist felt that persons subscribing fervently to such a supernatural hypothesis "undoubtedly contributed in a significant way to discrediting the UFO problem."

But you may be wondering, "How so?" In answering that question, Dr. McDonald declared that, "Cultist and crackpot ideas abound in a garish 'literature' of paperbacks and magazine articles.... This all-too-visible group is frequently identified by scientists as constituting the totality of those who take seriously the UFO problem. To lump serious students of the UFO together with the cultist-crackpot fringe is an error that results simply from limiting one's examination to a superficial, armchair approach to the UFO record. One can, in fact, easily and quickly separate the crackpots from the serious investigators."

Dr. McDonald truly regretted that so few scientists had yet taken the trouble to carry out such a sifting process.

The editors of *UFO Contact*, Ronald Caswell in the United Kingdom and Major H. C. Petersen in Denmark, were openly puzzled as to why Dr. McDonald was submitting articles for publication to them and sharing information on his scientific UFO investigations. *UFO Contact*, after all, was the official publication of the International Get Acquainted Program (IGAP), whose very purpose of existence was stated to be a dissemination of "the philosophy brought to the world by Mr. George Adamski" as an aid in helping humankind uncover the truth of its celestial origin and future destiny among the stars.

George Adamski was the most prominent contactee in the 1950s and the first half of the 1960s. He maintained that the Venusians and other extraterrestrials were here on Earth, living and working clandestinely, for the express purpose of saving us from ourselves. Our development of fissionable nuclear devices, along with our continued progress in fabricating the technology to deliver such deadly payloads, threatened the continued existence of all life on Earth, as well as the destabilization of the orbits of the planets within our solar system. Since Dr. McDonald had previously pinpointed some contactees who had spoken about "Space Brothers from Venus, Mars and Saturn" coming here to save us from such hazards, as being "cultists," Caswell and Major Petersen questioned, "Are we among the 'crackpots' and 'cultists' of Dr. James E. McDonald? Are we of the lunatic fringe?"

The editors answered this rhetorical question by asking the readers of *UFO Contact* to look through all of the back issues and see if they could find any articles in the magazine that give any indications of "cultish leanings." Caldwell and Major Petersen wrote, "Or has it not, time and again, brought forth strong evidence for its reasoning? Has it appeared as an eccentric magazine with no set purpose except a willy-nilly pushing of outer space contacts, or has it tried to bring inquiry where inquiry was needed, pressure where pressure should be brought to bear, in the interest of all?"

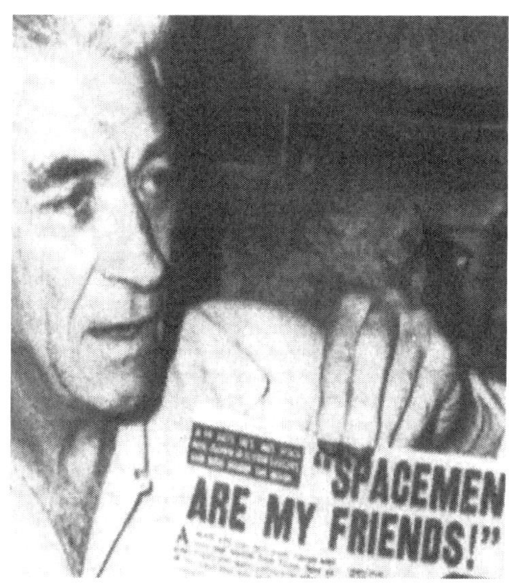

The "Cosmic Ray" Keller on George Adamski: "He was not a prophet, just delivering cosmic telegrams." Photo first appeared in Real magazine, special Flying Saucers Pictorial edition, 1967.

When Alan T. Weston and I co-edited the *Flying Saucer Report* in Bedford, Ohio, from 1967-1972, we exchanged publications and carried on a correspondence with Major Hans Petersen at the International Get Acquainted Program (IGAP). The magazine was always first-rate, in my estimation. Each issue of *UFO Contact* kept its international readership well informed in all aspects of the UFO phenomenon. George Adamski, in all of his writings, stressed the fact that his mission did not include the propagation of any new religion; and he made it a point for the attendees at his lectures and the readers of his books to stay in the ranks of their own religion and continue to strive and live up to its highest principles. Adamski also stressed that his extraterrestrial friends were not "space gods" and did not need for anyone to worship them, or pay them homage. He was not a prophet, just delivering cosmic telegrams. "And basically," emphasized the editors, "we have tried to do what George Adamski did during his lifetime: tell the world about flying saucers, entertain no ideological ideas, offer no nationalistic portrayal of events, and fear no man."

Dr. McDonald was himself a subscriber to my own *Flying Saucer Report*, however; so I know from correspondence with him, albeit from more than 50 years ago, that he did not lump Adamski in with some other contactees, who more or less described their encounters with extraterrestrials as having taken place on the psychic plane. Following his initial and physical contact with Orthon on 20 November 1952, out on the Mojave Desert, Adamski became more cautious with respect to any forms of psychic communication with space people.

According to the premier Swedish ufologist and foremost European authority on the contactee phenomenon, Hakan Blomqvist, it was well known that later in his life, Adamski "was very much against any form of psychic communication with space people and strongly objected to the esoteric interpretation of his physical contacts given by Meade Layne and Riley Crabb of Borderland Sciences Research Association (BSRA)." Be sure and see Hakan Blomqvist's blog, dated 29 October 2013, "George Adamski Correspondence," http://ufoarchives.blogspot.com/2013/10/the-george-adamski-correspondence.html. Although Adamski suspected there might be some kind of metaphysical interplay taking place in his encounters, he wasn't ready to fully commit himself to the explanations proffered by the BSRA contingent.

The two BSRA leaders regarded the craft and space people as belonging to a world in an ethereal dimension that was normally invisible to us. Adamski was relatively sure that his encounters occurred in the physical universe; but he wasn't quite ready to completely dismiss any possible metaphysical connection to his unique experiences. Moreover, given the subjective nature of the contactee conundrum, committing to the confining explanations of the BSRA would limit Adamski's options in interpreting it within his own cultural and personal context. That Adamski, Crabb and Layne were all members of the Theosophical Society decidedly shaped their philosophy with regard to the possible nature of extraterrestrial life; but this was no guarantee for the emergence of any consensus on the details of ultra-dimensionality.

Dr. James E. McDonald was intelligent enough to detect and respect these nuances. Insofar as Adamski was in the ballpark of a physical universe for the vast portion of his life as a contactee, and not caught up in living an illusion, then Dr. McDonald could make the time to work as a strong ally with the members of the IGAP. The IGAP membership honored the continuing legacy of George Adamski. Perhaps we should, as well.

As we continue on in this chapter, we will delve into the alliance of Dr. McDonald and Dr. Hynek in challenging the University of Colorado at Boulder's so-called *Scientific Study of Unidentified Flying Objects*, in addition to the unusual circumstances leading up to the alleged suicide of Dr. McDonald.

Scientists on Earth decipher a cosmic message of doom imparted from a mechanical intelligence on Venus. It was encrypted onto a cylinder found inside a spaceship that crashed in a taiga forest of Siberia. Scene above is from *First Spaceship on Venus* (1960), produced by the East German-Polish VEB Progress Film-Vertrieb and directed by Kurt Maetzig.

In the previous paragraphs, it was noted that Dr. James E. McDonald of the Meteorology Department of the University of Arizona at Tucson, began to have some misgivings, early on, about any degree of objectivity coming out of the then ongoing government-contracted University of Colorado at Boulder's so-called *Scientific Study of Unidentified Flying Objects*. This was popularly known as the Condon Report, because it was directed by the University of Colorado theoretical physicist, Dr. Edward Uhler Condon.

In 1966, following the so-called "swamp gas" sightings fiasco in Michigan, the United States Air Force reluctantly bowed to public opinion and invited the brilliant Dr. Condon, well known for both his candor and courage, to undertake an independent investigation of the UFO phenomenon. Unfortunately for the Air Force and all concerned, Dr. Condon made no secret, from the very outset of the $496,155 taxpayer-funded UFO investigation, that at least so far as he was concerned, "No substantive evidence for extraterrestrial visitation was liable to result." The study only lasted for two years, and for the most part, the American scientific community accepted the Condon committee's apparently negative conclusions about UFOs. With an immediate rubber stamp on the Condon Report from the National Academy of Sciences in 1968, the Air Force closed up shop on *Project Blue Book*, its official UFO investigation, in the following year.

At the 26 January 1968 seminar of the United Aircraft Research Laboratories in East Hartford, Connecticut, however, with a half a year of investigations still remaining for the University of Colorado UFO project, Dr. James E. McDonald sounded a rather pessimistic note. In Dr. McDonald's opinion, the Colorado group was "doing an entirely inadequate job" in its UFO study.

"Condon," said the Arizona professor of atmospheric physics, "is ignoring scientific reports and instead is concerned with the 'crackpot' and 'cultist' aspects. I am troubled by his whimsical preoccupation with the crackpot and cultist aspect of the UFO problem and his evident lack of attention to the scientific side." Dr. McDonald added that, "I find it difficult to justify his interest in the crackpot aspects to exclusion of consideration of reports of pilots, scientists, engineers, law enforcement officers, and all the credible witnesses whose testimony has been so impressive to most who have been willing to examine it firsthand."

It seems that Dr. McDonald's harsh criticism of the Condon Committee was being echoed from other unexpected quarters in the American scientific community. According to an article that appeared in the January-February 1968 edition of the National Investigations Committee on Aerial Phenomena (NICAP) *UFO Investigator*, none other than the Air Force's own *Project Blue Book* chief scientific consultant, Dr. J. Allen Hynek, declared that, "If the Colorado Project's conclusion is completely negative- denying the UFO reality- I will take the wraps off his personal files of good, unexplained cases and make them public."

The NICAP article noted that Dr. Hynek had investigated over one thousand UFO cases that he personally considered as "unresolved." Like Dr. Condon and Dr. McDonald, Dr. Hynek's specialty was physics, or astrophysics, to be more precise. Coupled with twenty years of investigating UFOs for the Air Force, one would certainly be impressed by anything concerning the phenomenon that Dr. Hynek would care to venture.

In the early months of 1968, Dr. Hynek was the director of the Dearborn Observatory in Chicago and was still serving as the *Project Blue Book* Chief UFO Consultant, a position he had held continuously for the past 18 years. While up to that time, Dr. Hynek was considered to be an absolute skeptic when it came to UFOs, he nevertheless could not just stand by and let the Condon Committee continue to hoodwink the American people in its subjective and unscientific approach to the subject of UFOs.

The truth about the Condon Committee was coming out. The *Colorado Daily* of Friday, 9 February 1968 reported that on the previous day, "Condon said David

As one of the Cosmic Ray's Venusian friends might say, "Let's face the facts about flying saucers!" See https://www.dollskill.com/o-mighty-ufos-crop-tee.html.

Saunders and Norman E. Levine were both notified Thursday 'of the termination of their positions on the staff of the project.'

"He (Condon) said the two men were dismissed because of incompetence, but refused further comment.

"Saunders was co-principal investigator for the project and Levine was a research associate.

"Neither Levine nor Saunders were available for comment. Also not available was UFO Project Director Robert Low."

Of this situation at Boulder, Dr. Hynek would later write: "Almost from the start, the Condon Committee ran into troubles. The foremost of these stemmed from the personalities of the director, Dr. Condon, and his chief administrator, the late Robert Low. These are detailed best in Dr. David Saunders' book, *UFOs?: Yes!* ,[26]and in less detail in my own book, *The UFO Experience.* [27] The committee never worked as a coherent body and was torn by much internal strife."

Hynek-McDonald Friendship Tested

Dennis Stacy was the editor of the prestigious *Mutual UFO Network Journal* from 1985 to 1997. During his first year in the capacity of *Journal* editor, Stacy secured an interview with Dr. Hynek, then known as the "Dean of Ufology." Dr. Hynek, being unusually frank in his responses to Stacy's questions, despite his twenty years experience with the Air Force, acknowledged his long-lasting friendship with Dr. James E. McDonald, and also pointed out those aspects of the Condon Report of which they failed to arrive at a consensus. The following is an excerpt from the Stacy-Hynek exchange:

STACY: What began to change your own perception of the UFO phenomenon?

HYNEK: Two things, really. One was the completely negative and unyielding attitude of the Air Force. They wouldn't give UFOs the chance of existing, even if they were flying up and down the street in broad daylight. Everything had to have an explanation. I began to resent that, even though I basically felt the same way, because I still thought they weren't going about it in the right way. You can't assume that everything is black no matter what. Secondly, the caliber of the witnesses began to trouble me. Quite a few instances were reported by military pilots, for example; and I knew them to be fairly well-trained; so this is when I first began to think that, well, maybe there's something to all this.

The famous "swamp gas" case, which came later on, finally pushed me over the edge. From that point on, I began to look at reports from a different angle, which was to say that some of them could be true UFOs.

STACY: As your own attitude changed, did the Air Force's attitude toward you change, too?

HYNEK: It certainly did, quite a bit, as a matter of fact. By way of background, I might add that the late Dr. James E. McDonald, a good friend of mine who was then an atmospheric meteorologist at the University of Arizona, and I had some fairly sharp words about it. He used to accuse me very much, saying, "You're the scientific consultant to the Air Force. You should be pounding on generals' doors and insisting on getting a better job done."

---

26 David R. Saunders and R. Roger Harkins, *UFOs?: Yes!* (New York: New American, Library, 1968)

27 J. Allen Hynek, *The UFO Experience* (London: Abelard-Schuman, Limited, 1972)

I said, "Jim, I was there. You weren't. You don't know the mindset. They were under instruction from the Pentagon, following the Robertson Panel of 1953, that the whole subject had to be debunked, period, no question about it. That was the prevailing attitude. The panel was convened by the CIA; and I sat in on it; but I was not asked to sign the resolution. Had I been asked, I would not have signed it, because they took a completely negative attitude about everything."

So when Jim McDonald used to accuse me of a sort of miscarriage of scientific justice, I had to tell him that if I had done what he wanted, the generals would not have listened to me. They were already listening to Dr. Donald Menzel and the other boys over at the Harvard Astronomy Department as it was.

Someone stole Dr. McDonald's briefcase from an airplane and then walked off with his slides for a UFO lecture. He was under constant surveillance by intelligence operatives following his investigation of a flying saucer incident at the China Lake Naval Weapons Station out in the California desert. See http://jeremyvarner.com/blog/2017/10/the-real-men-in-black/.

Dr. Menzel, it should be well noted, was the world's premier UFO skeptic before the arrival of Dr. Edward U. Condon and the publication of his University of Colorado study.

Red Flags Go Up

Following the release of the nearly 1,500 page *Condon Report*, Dr. McDonald carefully poured over its contents, looking for every discrepancy he could find. He immediately hit the lecture circuit, speaking out against Dr. Edward U. Condon and his biased study at every opportunity afforded him, at civilian UFO groups, fraternal organizations, radio and television programs, and university lecture halls. He urged his audiences to rally Congress and support increased federal funding for the investigation of UFO reports. The physicist also wrote a series of magazine and newspaper articles about the reality of UFOs, noting that many of the cold case UFO reports in the *Condon Report* might be revisited by a team of more objective scientists from a wider variety of specialties.

It was about this time that everything started to "go south" in Dr. McDonald's life. Friends, as well as work associates at the university, began to notice some erratic behaviors and personality quirks. Dr. McDonald was having an extremely difficult time in dealing with the public ridicule coming in his direction from some of his colleagues in the scientific community. This barrage of denunciation was focused exclusively on the doctor's pro-stance with regard to the reality of UFOs and his suggestions that some of the reports of these ever elusive objects might be attributable to the visitation of extraterrestrial spaceships.

In May 1969, Dr. McDonald suddenly dropped out of his California lecture tour and returned to his home in Tucson, Arizona. While he was lecturing in the evenings out in California, he was investigating a series of UFO sightings that occurred around the China Lake Naval Air Weapons Station during the day. Apparently, he uncovered something spectacular and needed to get back to the university to conduct further research on it in the laboratory facilities there. But during the flight home, his briefcase disappeared. It was chock-full of sensitive, taped interviews and documents related to some fantastic event that took place out on the desert at China Lake.

Everyone around Dr. McDonald began to think he was becoming paranoid. He insisted that almost everywhere he went, he was being followed by men in dark suits driving unmarked cars, without license plates. His wife, Betsy, was known as a social activist and supporter of many leftist and revolutionary causes. At one time, Betsy even had two leaders of the Black Panther Party for Self-Defense from Oakland, California over at their home while they were giving a discourse in the Political Science Department at the university. At that time, the McDonalds had noted that the militants appeared to be under surveillance by government intelligence operatives, but they themselves had never been approached for questioning. Dr. McDonald was sure that he was being tailed and dogged by the government, however, for an entire carousel of valuable UFO slides had been taken from the projector at one of his bigger speaking engagements out on the East Coast.

All of this pressure was too much for Betsy; and in March 1971, she filed for a divorce. On top of the doctor's inclinations toward paranoia, Betsy was feeling neglected due to her husband's many trips and long hours away from home. Dr. McDonald was then at the breaking point. On 9 April 1971, the physicist made an unsuccessful attempt at taking his own life, shooting himself in the head with a pistol, severing an optic nerve and leaving him partially blind. He soldiered on, however, and returned to work and UFO investigations.

The pistol that Dr. McDonald had used in the initial suicide attempt had been confiscated by the police. On 12 June 1971, however, the doctor took a taxi cab from his university office to a pawn shop in downtown Tucson, where he purchased a .38 caliber revolver. That was the last time that anyone had seen of Dr. McDonald alive. On the next day there was a family walking along a creek that came across his body under the Canada Del Oro Bridge spanning a wash in Tucson.

Interestingly, in between Dr. McDonald's two suicide attempts, one of America's top ufologists wrote a piece for the May 1971 edition of *Saga* magazine entitled "Liquidation of the UFO Investigators." Perhaps Otto O. Binder penned this piece in light of Dr. McDonald's failed try, which had so caught the attention of the world's ufology community.

In the groundbreaking article, Binder noted that, "All of this is not meant to frighten anyone who takes an active part in the UFO field. In fact, another and very startling viewpoint can be taken in regard to the 'premature' deaths of the ufologists.

"Can it be than when such important 'UFO evangelists' as Frank Edwards, Morris K. Jessup, Mark Probert, and others have 'fulfilled their task' in behalf of 'preaching' ufology, they are 'taken away' deliberately for their own sake? That is, having met the scorn and blind opposition of the unheeding world long enough, are they then mercifully removed from the 'battlefront?'

"This, you see," explained Binder, "puts a different light on the deaths of ufologists. Maybe they are being rewarded, not punished. Maybe they are 'taken within the fold.' Who knows?"

Something was afoot accounting for the higher death rate among ufologists. Binder was sure of this. "That something," wrote Binder, "may either be the secret machinations of the UFO hierarchy who decides which Earth people 'know too much about flying saucers,' or the planned removal of UFO crusaders who have done their job nobly. Take your choice…."

Many thanks for your magnificent work, Dr. McDonald. I'm sure you've finally found your happy place among the twinkling stars. –Cosmic Ray

For an outstanding biography of Dr. McDonald, your attention is invited to Ann Druffel, *Firestorm: Dr. James E. McDonald's Fight for UFO Science* (Columbus, North Carolina: Wild Flower Press, 2003).

Chapter 8: The Moon Is a Venusian Colony

ТАКОГО ЕЩЕ НЕ БЫЛО!

СОВЕТСКАЯ ЛАБОРАТОРИЯ ДЕЙСТВУЕТ НА ЛУНЕ

ЧЕЛОВЕК

ИЗВЕСТИЯ

СОВЕТОВ ДЕПУТАТОВ ТРУДЯЩИХСЯ СССР

«ЛУНА-9» ПЕРЕДАЕТ ИЗОБРАЖЕНИЕ ЛУННОЙ ПОВЕРХНОСТИ

Soviet newspaper *Izvestiya*, 5 February 1966, announces successful landing of Luna 9 robotic spacecraft on surface of the Moon.

Soviet Moon Probe

It's hard to believe that next year will mark the fiftieth anniversary for humankind's taking of its first steps on the Moon, the nearest celestial body to the Earth. Just three years before the historic Moon landing of the American Apollo 11 landing vehicle, space scientists the world over were still trying to figure out what the lunar surface was largely composed of.

Patriotic contactees like George Adamski and Howard Menger, who had been to the Moon courtesy of the Venusians, told personnel of the National Aeronautics and Space Administration (NASA) working on the proposed Moon shot that our astronauts would have nothing to fear in that regard, that they would find a hard and safe surface to walk on.

Perhaps the NASA scientists and technicians working on the Apollo program already knew about the lunar surface conditions; but they didn't want to share that information with the Soviet scientists. After all, we Americans were in a race against time with the Soviets to put the first astronauts on the Moon and return them safely to Earth. If the Soviets wanted to know about the lunar surface, the head honchos at NASA probably decided it would be better if they wasted their own time and money to figure it all out. Why cut them any slack, and give them a leg up on us in the ongoing space race?

Just one month into 1966, the Soviet Union did just that. On 31 January the Soviet space program successfully launched their Luna 9 probe. It "soft landed" on the Moon on 3 February by employing its powerful retro-thrust braking rockets to set the 3,200 pound craft gently down. Of course, the Soviets amazed the entire world with this landing. Americans were beginning to wonder if NASA was going to maintain fidelity with the late president John F. Kennedy's stated ambition for the United States of America to put the first astronauts on the Moon.

With the Luna 9, it was clear that the Soviets had taken a significant leap ahead of us in the space race. What was even more impressive was that the Luna 9 probe, after landing without any problems, was able to deploy a television camera and send live photos from the surface of the Moon. One of the biggest discoveries about the Moon revealed by this television transmission was the firm ground that the spacecraft touched down upon. This literally served to explode the famous theory of a dust-covered lunar surface in which any space vehicles would simply sink out of sight (Otto Binder, "Our Space Age" syndicated panels, 28 and 30 March 1966, Bell-McClure Syndicate, *Paterson News*, New Jersey).

Lunar "Pyramids" and "Spikes"

It became more than obvious that if the American populace and taxpayers were going to continue to stand behind NASA's efforts to land astronauts on the Moon, that something should be done to at least catch up with, and maybe outdo, the Soviet Union's great accomplishment in landing the Luna 9 on the Moon's surface. The big breakthrough was revealed on Tuesday, 22 November 1966, when scientists at the Jet Propulsion Laboratory (JPL) in Pasadena, California, declared that their own Lunar Orbiter 2 had taken photographs of what appeared to be "pyramids on the Moon," along with other "spike-like objects or obelisks that bore a remarkable resemblance to the Washington Monument."

This is an artist's conception of the United States Lunar Orbiter 2 discovery of strange pyramid and spike formations on the lunar surface. Source: Argosy magazine, August 1970.

A spokesperson for the JPL announced that, "Unusual mounds that appear like tall, skinny pyramids" turned up in one of the photographs among the first batches of the Lunar Orbiter 2 photographs. The photograph with the pyramids was enlarged five times and showed an area of about 750-by-550 feet. It represented the fourth of 13 potential landing sites for American astronauts slotted for exploring the lunar surface. The unique photograph was forwarded to NASA by the JPL. A spokesman for NASA noted that the area in question had about "six protuberances with the largest appearing to be about 50 feet wide at the base and 40-to-75 feet high." The spokesman added that, "Some of the smaller ones look like upside down ice cream cones. I've never seen anything like it before."

By way of explanation, the NASA spokesman declared that, "At the same time that the Orbiter 2 was photographing the area, the Sun was about 11 degrees above the lunar horizon during the sunrise phase of the Moon's two-week long 'day.' This accounts for the long shadows," the spokesman asserted, hoping that his conjecture would suffice for the members of the press corps present for his Lunar Orbiter 2 mission briefing. The spokesman rambled on: "The striking shadow-casting protuberances are naturally occurring features on the lunar surface. They looked indigenous to the Moon and are spaced at random." He also stated that a "determination of the precise height of the protuberances would only be possible after ground slope measurements had been made," additionally noting that, "Some of the smaller protuberances in the cratered upland basin in the area called the Sea of Tranquility appeared weather beaten and rounded."

The source for this information was a United Press International (UPI) report dated 22 November 1966, as published in the Wednesday, 23 November 1966 edition of the Philadelphia, Pennsylvania, *Inquirer* newspaper. Remember, this was almost three years before the launch of the Apollo 11 mission, whose destination was ultimately designated as the Sea of Tranquility, the location of these strange lunar protuberances and domes. Clearly, NASA officials were desirous to find out the true nature of these structures. It is doubtful they accepted the first premise offered of them being something "indigenous" to the Moon and "spaced at random" insofar as the true height of each object could not be determined. Some of the objects were also purely conical in shape while others resembled obelisks. These are not naturally occurring shapes.

Some kind of fervent activity appeared to be taking place on the Moon. It might signal extraterrestrial construction on our own supposed "natural" satellite. Keep reading this chapter wherein Dr. Raymond Keller reveals other unique lunar phenomena and demonstrates how the strange protuberances on the Moon actually stumped all of the JPL and NASA's so-called lunar "experts." Learn what key figures in the international ufology community were saying as NASA was preparing to launch the Apollo 11 and American astronauts would walk on the surface of the Moon. You can be sure our explorers were not alone up there.

Pioneer ufologist and UFO photographer, August C. Roberts, is pictured above. August believed the Apollo Moon missions would reveal much about our mysterious Moon. Photos courtesy of Rense Radio, with second photo first appearing in 4 July 1969 issue of Allentown, Pennsylvania Morning Call newspaper, in Keller Venus files.

The contactees of the 1950s and early 1960s tried to tell us that the Moon was already colonized by extraterrestrials, mostly Venusians. August C. Roberts, a close associate of the New Jersey sign painter and contactee, Howard Menger, who claimed to have taken a ride to a Venusian base on the Moon in a flying saucer, was interviewed by Joan Wiessmann, a correspondent for the *Morning Call* newspaper of Allentown, Pennsylvania. The intriguing interview appeared in the Friday, 4 July 1969 edition of the newspaper, just two weeks and two days before astronaut Neil Armstrong became the first man to walk on the surface of the Moon. Wiessmann's interview with Roberts is important because it reflected the then extant mindset of most ufologists about the space program and a perceived cover-up of the truth about the UFO phenomenon.

In the Wiessmann article entitled "Augie Wants Moon News," Roberts is quoted as saying that, "The Moon landing should prove a lot of things. It will also prove some people liars."

At the time of the interview, Roberts was living in Wayne Township, New Jersey. Roberts could hardly contain his enthusiasm for the projected 20 July Moon landing. He was anxious to see if the astronauts would find dome-like buildings on the surface of the Moon. Roberts was a photographer noted for his tremendous collection of UFO pictures. But the finest flying saucer photos in his collection came from his good friend, the contactee Howard Menger. The famous photographer explained that, "I know a chap, Howard Menger, who has some good pictures of what he claims are flying saucers." Roberts added that, "Menger claims to have been on the Moon. I did a book with him titled '*From Outer Space to You*.'" This book was published by the Saucerian Press of Clarksburg, West Virginia, in 1959.

Roberts continued: "Menger says some people from Venus landed in his backyard at High Bridge, New Jersey, and took him for a ride to the Moon." While Menger was hovering over the Moon in a Venusian scout ship, the pilot of the craft allowed him to take some photographs of dome-like buildings on the lunar surface. These he turned over to his friend and fellow UFO researcher August C. Roberts, long acknowledged as one of the world's leading authorities when it came to taking photographs of unexplained aerial and space phenomena.

Enter Valiant Thor

Of Menger, Roberts commented that, "I know his story very well. I believe that Menger thinks he is telling the truth; but I don't necessarily believe the story." When reporter Wiessmann asked Roberts to elaborate on this, Roberts explained that once he was in attendance at a meeting where the sign painter, Menger, was addressing the members of a flying saucer club assembled at his High Bridge home. Menger allegedly told the membership that there was a man from Venus among them, although they weren't quite sure who he was.

"I took pictures of an unusual-looking man and then had these reproduced," said Roberts, also declaring that, "Nobody has stepped forward and disproved the story. Menger called him Valiant Thor." These and other photographs from Roberts' special collection have been widely publicized in almost every UFO journal ever since. Just recently, I published them along with Roberts' official seal and typed comments as found on the back of each photograph on the Jeff Rense Radio website.

Back in 1969, most of Roberts' photos remained in his "secret file," then considered one of the largest archives of UFO pictures in the entire United States, if not the world. Those photographs of UFOs and alleged extraterrestrials not taken by Roberts were carefully copied by him from other special collections. Roberts also co-produced a full-length commercial movie about flying saucers with Dr. Frank Stranges, out in Van Nuys, California. The movie was a UFO documentary entitled, "*Phenomena 7-7*."

August C. Roberts was musing prophetic when he declared that, "What I do today, the children of tomorrow will see in books and movies." Now, 49 years later, prominent Hollywood movie director Craig Campobasso has succeeded in garnering sufficient financing to go ahead with the production of a full-blown feature film about Valiant Thor's arrival and activities here on Earth from 1957-1960. The movie will be titled *Stranger in the Pentagon* and should be in theaters sometime late next year or into the beginning of 2020.

Roberts on the *Condon Report*

During the time of the interview, the United States government recently concluded an exhaustive study of UFOs. It was contracted to the University of Colorado at Boulder and headed up by the prominent physicist Dr. Edward U. Condon. The Colorado team was assigned the task of determining whether or not flying saucers as extraterrestrial spacecraft were actually coming to the Earth. The Air Force paid the University of Colorado slightly over $500,000 to study this matter in 1966; and the study formally concluded in November 1968. Their report, titled *Scientific Study of Unidentified Flying Objects*, was released in January 1969. It has commonly come to be known as the *Condon Report*. Of the final document, Roberts was not impressed. "The research group must be incompetent because they decided the saucers didn't exist," he assured Wiessmann.

The pioneering ufologist added that, "I have proof-positive that they do exist. The people never asked to look at my files. The flying saucers look like bell-type ships."

Wiessmann wondered if Roberts had any problems with the government, being so knowledgeable about the flying saucers traversing our skies. The ufologist did admit that he was once escorted out of the Pentagon because he and a companion called out some top government officials as "liars" with respect to some of their misleading remarks about the UFO phenomenon that they were making to the press.

"They told us that President Ike Eisenhower said the UFOs were only sunspots," noted Roberts. He thought this was a dubious statement because he served as a plane spotter at a remote base of the Army Air Corps situated at a secret location in a mountainous section along the Mexican border in 1943. "At that time, I and the other enlisted men were amazed to see a huge orange object circle below us in the valley. I know what a sunspot looks like, and this object exhibited no resemblance to that type of phenomenon."

Remarkable Career

In his long career in the burgeoning subject of ufology, Roberts noted that for 1969, the year of the Moon shot, "business is slow these days as far as UFOs are concerned." He added that, "A few UFOs have been seen in foreign countries. But you know, the saucers are supposed to appear in cycles. I believe it's every five years." Roberts expounded on the close approach of Mars and other planets in the solar system, when UFO activity seems to peak. "But I don't say this is true. I don't subscribe to any space theory." Like the great anomalist John A. Keel, who worked in close association with Roberts on several projects, the prominent UFO photographer thought that there might be some inter-dimensional aspect to the whole UFO scenario, although he couldn't be sure. "I keep an open mind to the possibility of UFOs as coming from some unseen ultra-dimensional reality," he declared.

Another prolific figure from the UFO community who worked with Roberts was Gray Barker, the publisher of the Saucerian Press in Clarksburg, West Virginia. Barker edited and published Howard Menger's first book, *From Outer Space to You*. Barker also popularized the frequent appearance of the mysterious Men in Black to UFO experiencers. Barker accused these dark figures with silencing the voices of those participating in close encounters of the third kind, or contact with the flying saucer occupants, and thereby keeping the truth about UFOs from the public at large. But it was Gray Barker who said of Roberts that, "If anybody deserves to be honored as a flying saucer pioneer, that person is August C. Roberts. In the unfolding saucer drama, his name has become as familiar as those of George Adamski, Major Donald E. Keyhoe, Ray Palmer and others."

Roberts served as photographic consultant for Gray Barker's Saucerian Press, in addition to working for a time with Raymond Palmer and his line of mystic, flying saucer, science fiction and space magazines. Long associated with UFO contactee Dominick Lucchesi, also of New Jersey, they published one of the very first flying saucer magazines, Nexus. He has given assistance to practically every major researcher from the early days of ufology, and was doing the photographic layout on a UFO book with comic book, science fiction and space writer Otto Binder, right before Binder passed away in 1974 at his Chestertown, New York, home.

One of the most exciting moments in Roberts' UFO career took place in 1952. He was positioned in a sky watch tower and actually snapped a photo of a saucer which appeared directly above New York City. The photograph was shown on television, in newspapers up and down the East Coast, and national magazines. Roberts even appeared on a major television news program in 1955 where he displayed the photograph, along with some others of UFOs that he had taken since 1952 on other occasions. His account of the sighting and photograph of the object, along with other UFO photos, were included in the Westinghouse time capsule buried at the conclusion of the 1964 New York World's Fair. The capsule will not be opened until the year 6939. Hopefully, UFO disclosure will have come by then. But I suppose we shouldn't hold our breath.

Another Moon Mystery

The discovery of mysterious obelisk and domed structures in the mountains to the north of the Sea of Tranquility on the surface of the Moon cinched the area as the first priority landing zone for the Apollo 11's lunar excursion module. Astronomers at the Corralitos Observatory on a remote ranch in the desert north of Las Cruces, New Mexico, attached there by a special lunar phenomena investigations division of Northwestern University in Evanston, Illinois, were conducting a survey of the mountains and craters in and around the Sea of Tranquility just weeks prior to the Apollo 11 launch, when they reported a unique ultraviolet radiation in close vicinity to the proposed landing zone.

Back in July 1969, while co-editing the *Flying Saucer Report* out of Bedford, Ohio, I received a newspaper clipping from a subscriber in Arizona. It was dated 5 July 1969 and first appeared as an Associated Press dispatch in the Tucson *Daily Citizen*. Titled, "Scientists Find a Moon Mystery," this news item detailed how a group of New Mexico astronomers recorded intermittent fluxes of radiation from a large crater not far from the proposed Tranquility landing site. They had been monitoring this radiation flux for the past two years. "We are detecting in the Aristarchus region on a lunar monthly basis an excess of blue or ultraviolet," noted J. R. Dunlap, the resident director of the observatory.

Threat Assessment

President Richard M. Nixon was apprised of the situation at Aristarchus crater directly by Dunlap. "What you are telling me is certainly unprecedented, Dunlap. That this radiation threat is centered so close to our designated Apollo landing zone is worrisome to me. Do you think we should temporarily postpone the mission?" inquired Nixon.

The Corralitos facility director replied that, "Mr. President, I do not believe the radiation will threaten the Apollo 11 astronauts or future Moon landing crews."

"Would it be prudent to select an alternate landing site?" asked the president.

Dunlap declared that, "I think that I should defer to the head of our astronomy department at Northwestern University for that, Dr. J. Allen Hynek. We are definitely dealing with something quite extraordinary at Aristarchus and the Tranquility region in general."

"Yes, I know Hynek. I've consulted him before on similar occurrences in outer space," remarked Nixon.

Hynek Briefs Nixon

The president's secretary set up a secure telephone line for Nixon to speak directly to Hynek at Northwestern. The following is a summation of their conversation.

Nixon: Dr. Hynek, what's going on at Aristarchus crater? We're getting too close to launch with Apollo 11 to start making any mission deviations.

Hynek: From what my people at Corralitos are telling me, their observations of the ultraviolet radiation began while they were in the process of searching for information about some of the centuries-old phenomena on the Moon that have long baffled us in the astronomy community.

Nixon: What are we talking about here, Hynek? I know you're my "Johnny on the Spot" for everything UFOs and paranormal. Are we talking about ET activity on the Moon? Don't B.S. me, Hynek. I'm not John Q. Public that's going to buy off on "swamp gas" or "Venus seen in some weather inversion," or any other lame explanation, for that matter.

Hynek: I'd never B.S. you, Mr. President. You were right there in the White House when our first emissary showed up there. So there's no bull shitting you, Mr. President.

Nixon: Glad we have that settled. So what's up at this crater that I should know about?

Hynek: Our folks at Corralitos were charged by me to monitor the areas where this "red glow" has been consistently observed. I wanted them to watch for any such red glows in the area where our astronauts are planning to land.

Nixon: That seems wise, Hynek. Please continue.

Hynek: Well, these red glowing areas on the Moon have been observed by astronomers for at least four centuries. They're called lunar transient events. But besides the red glow, our astronomers at Corralitos and other telescopes devoted to lunar observations have reported seeing temporary increases in the brightness at Aristarchus crater. It has changed colors in its pulsating brightness.

Nixon: We have our reasons to suspect saucer activity on the back side of the Moon; but I wasn't aware of anything taking place on the side that always faces us.

Hynek: This is a definite concern, Mr. President, especially in light of the fact that it's occurring now, right before our astronauts take off for that very region.

Nixon: So what have astronomers been doing about it? What more have you discovered, that I need to know about?

Hynek: As of a few days ago, the red glows have ceased. But they have been replaced by some quite pronounced emissions of ultraviolet radiation. Utilizing our 24-inch telescope at Corralitos, we couldn't be sure if the atmosphere or something was interfering to produce it; and we could not duplicate our findings. Frankly, Mr. President, I'm not sure just what the hell is going on up there.

Nixon: Dr. Hynek, given the unusual energy fluxes at Tranquility Base as reported from Corralitos, is it your opinion that we need to change our landing zone to somewhere else?

Hynek: I think we will be OK to stick with Tranquility Base as our LZ. The radiation has been observed regularly since last fall. We have no doubt that the radiation is there. Something, or someone, is causing it. I don't think we'll be alone up there on the Moon. It might be prudent to keep our astronauts apprised of this. ET will allow us to land and make our observations. But anything we find out about their presence on the Moon will have to be hushed up. As news of some strange lights and radiation near Aristarchus have already reached the ears of some in the news media, I suggest we go with a press release declaring something like, "The lunar rocks are just giving off a natural fluorescence, akin to the same process that causes mineral specimens in museums to glow under ultraviolet or infrared light."

Nixon: Do you really think the public is going to believe that?

Hynek: I certainly hope so. We are entering a new age with our Moon landing. ET may let us land on the Moon; but I doubt they will let us establish a continuing presence there.

The Aftermath

Dr. J. Allen Hynek, Astronomy Department director, Northwestern University, Evanston, Illinois, at time of Apollo 11 Moon landing. See https://www.imdb.com/name/nm0405251/.

President Richard M. Nixon was in his first year in office when the United States became the first nation to land men on the Moon and return them safely to Earth.

Following the success of the Apollo 11 Moon landing mission, both Dr. J. Allen Hynek and President Richard M. Nixon were asked for their opinions about extraterrestrials and UFOs at various news conferences. According to a 22 April 2009 article in the London, United Kingdom, *Telegraph* newspaper, this is what these two historic personages had to say on the matter:

Dr. J. Allen Hynek: "When the long-awaited solution to the UFO problem comes, I believe that it will prove to be not merely the next small step in the march of science, but a mighty and totally unexpected quantum leap. We had a job to do, whether right or wrong, to keep the public from getting excited."

President Richard M. Nixon, in office 1969-1974: "I'm not at liberty to discuss the government's knowledge of extraterrestrial UFOs at this time. I am still personally being briefed on the subject."

Viking Probes to Mars a Diversion

By the time that the United States Bicentennial was being celebrated in 1976, the world's attention towards all matters extraterrestrial had been diverted to the Viking 1 and 2 Mars missions, which were scheduled to land on the Red Planet on 20 July and 3 September, respectively, of that year. The Viking probes were to scoop up Martian dirt and then heat it up in built-in ovens to determine whether or not microorganisms existed there. The results were inconclusive. Some were suggesting, however, that the Viking missions were just a diversion for keeping us from more closely observing strange occurrences taking place on the Moon, just short of 250,000 miles away versus Mars, that is, on average, about 140 million miles away.

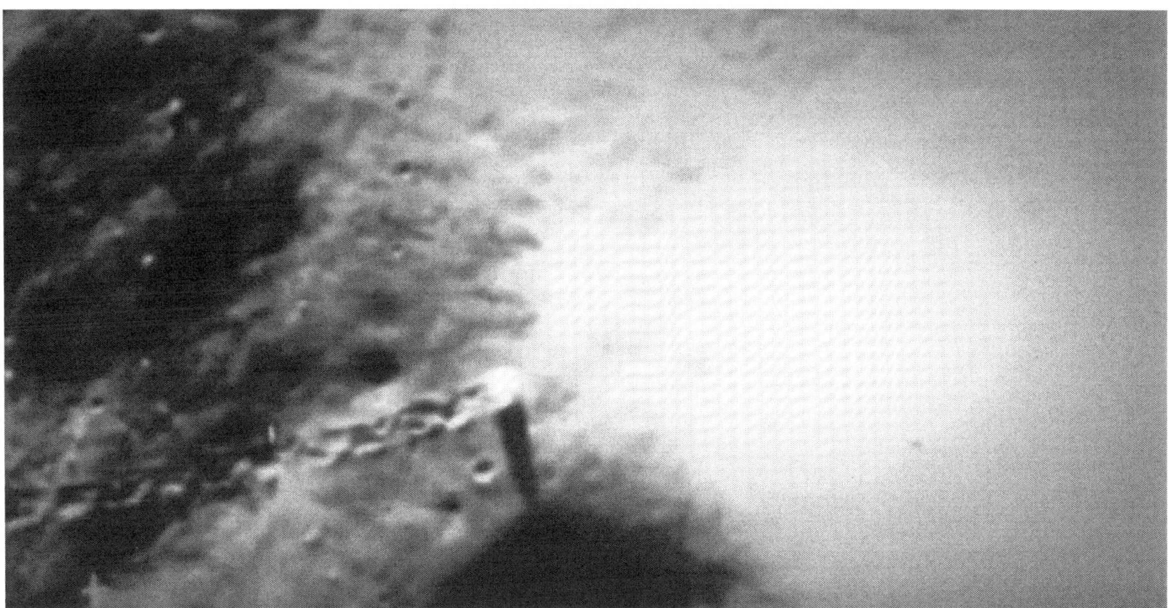

Tracks lead to a spire near crater rim on the Moon. Photo from National Geographic magazine 2015 television documentary, "Aliens on the Moon." Apollo 17 was launched on 17 December 1972 and was allegedly the last manned mission to the Moon. There are rumors of an Apollo 18 mission, where astronauts encountered extraterrestrials and were given a warning to take back to authorities on Earth, delineating areas of the Moon where future explorers were prohibited entry.

The Moon is Inhabited

In the seven years since the Apollo 11 mission, most Americans had moved on from paying even the slightest attention to the Moon, but not all. One of these consistently observing our closest celestial neighbor was former National Aeronautics and Space Administration (NASA) scientist and photographic analyst, the Harvard engineering graduate George H. Leonard. Making some pretty shocking claims about the Moon, Leonard backed these up by securing the original, massive prints of sundry classified photos taken by the various Apollo mission teams while in orbit or carrying out a reconnaissance of the lunar surface by foot or Moon buggy.

Leonard kept asserting that the Moon is inhabited. He compiled his photos in a wonderful book, *Somebody Else Is on the Moon* (Philadelphia, Pennsylvania: David McKay Company, Inc., 1976). Leonard's book opened a floodgate. Many NASA personnel, currently employed, fired, or retired, came forward to declare that everything stated in *Somebody Else Is on the Moon* was thoroughly accurate. They were just sorry that they didn't have the courage that Leonard displayed. They wished they had come out with full disclosures about what they had discovered about the Moon a lot sooner.

Despite official denials since hurled against Leonard and his book, the author accomplished much more than just spinning a fanciful theory. His exhaustive study and analysis of thousands of sundry Apollo missions' Moon photographs presents a convincing case that not only does the Moon have life on it, but that it is inhabited by intelligent beings that arrived there long ago from other planets, both inside and outside of our solar system, and colonized it for the express purpose of monitoring the spiritual and technological progress of humankind down through the ages.

Leonard maintains that the evidence for the presence of alien beings on our Moon is everywhere to be found: on the surface, on the far side and near side, in the craters, in the *maria* (Latin for "seas," but here indicative of vast lunar plains) and even in the lunar highlands. He believes that the extraterrestrials on the Moon have literally been changing its face with various construction projects underway for the longest, but undetermined times. Leonard held a sneaking suspicion that astronomical discoveries, like those mentioned in this series, triggered both the United States and Soviet Union's Moon programs. They may really be not so much the manifestation of a space race as a "desperate cooperation."

In Leonard's book, extensive attention is paid to photographs of the mysterious structures mentioned in the beginning of this chapter. There is also a photograph of a massive piece of machinery measuring five miles in diameter. The object in question is clearly a machine, because gears and teeth are visible. Leonard speculated that if the Moon machine were dropped down on Manhattan, it would literally "obliterate everything from midtown to the bowery." There are also huge "super-rigs" and "X-drones." Apparently, these are employed in moving significant amounts of lunar regolith. In the photos, these mechanisms seem to be knocking down ridge lines, carving away at the rim of craters, and more or less altering the very shape of the lunar landscape.

There are also strange sprays of dirt, sand, and even water that have been seen and photographed spewing out from craters. Leonard wonders what else might be emerging from the Moon's many craters. Similar sprays have been observed on Saturn's small moon of Enceladus and Neptune's largest natural satellite Triton. This orb is so big that astronomers speculate it is not a moon at all, but was once a planet on the edge of the Kuiper Belt that was captured by the gravitational pull of Neptune countless eons ago. These sprays on our Moon, Enceladus and Triton seem to be indicative of aquifers or underground seas, possible sources for extraterrestrial life.

It's not just Leonard's word versus the assertions of the whole NASA establishment that the Moon is a dead, lifeless orb. Leonard presents his readers with official photographs along with line drawings that help us to select the more intriguing details that he discovered, pinpointing the areas and features that have long puzzled astronomers and others in the world scientific community. NASA Plate 14 (designated 67-H-1135) clearly shows two long trails, 900 and 1,200 feet long. The objects that made these tracks are light-splashed by the Sun; so some details are blocked out. However, they clearly do not look like boulders or anything else in the surrounding area of the photograph.

Leonard speculates, "Do you know how much force it would take to set in motion a rock 75 feet across? Volcanic action might do it; but we have NASA's word for the fact that the Moon, on the surface at least, is seismically quiet." The engineer further explains that, "The smaller object in the photo- the one making the longer trail- came up out of a crater before it continued down the hill. Repeat: It came up out of a crater."

The former NASA engineer also points out a "fascinating tread mark on the trail of one of the 'boulders.' There is also a symmetrical design on the 'boulder' itself."

Two Engineers Share Moon Data

In my opinion, this Leonard's *Somebody Else Is on the Moon* is one of the more important books that the ufologist should maintain in her or his personal research library. I know for a fact that many persons inside of NASA helped Leonard obtain the hard-to-find and often classified information that he needed to write this fantastic book of Moon revelations. He mentions one engineer with a doctorate in physics, informed on all aspects of the Moon missions and lunar and the obstacles that our astronauts would encounter in the lunar geology. Leonard dubs him with the pseudonym of Dr. Samuel Wittcomb. What follows is the summation of a conversation between Leonard and Wittcomb.

Leonard: What did you mean when you said the Moon had "giant tailors?"

Wittcomb: Well, you see a lot of wreckage on the Moon, don't you?

Leonard: Agreed.

Wittcomb: That wreckage could have taken place a thousand years ago or millions of years ago.

Leonard: Right. But what does this mean?

Wittcomb: One argument the people use for the occupation-eons-ago theory is just that many of the artifacts we see are part of the wreckage. It's easy to believe there were aliens once on the Moon, pulling big pieces together- and they weren't finished?

Leonard: It would seem logical, then, that they are still around. They are still repairing. But where is it taking place?

Wittcomb: Several places, but I am surprised that you have not found them. Someone in the Jet Propulsion Lab (JPL) sketched some out for me. But I already knew they were there.

Of course, the engineer Leonard kept up his own investigation and found many more lunar anomalies on his own. One can appreciate *Somebody Else Is on the Moon* for its very capacity to cut through the official smokescreen surrounding our nearest celestial neighbor, opening our minds to an enigma of historic and profound proportions.

Some who have sought out this information under the Freedom of Information Act have run into brick walls. Here are the comments from the field investigator of a major UFO group, retired United States Army Command Sergeant Major Robert Dean at the Exopolitics Summit in Barcelona, Spain, in 2009:

> "Ladies and gentlemen, my government, NASA, which many of us in the United States say stands for *Never A Straight Answer*, proceeded to erase 40 rolls of film of the Apollo Program — the flight to the Moon, the flight around the Moon, the landings on the Moon, the walking guys here and there. They erased, for Christ's sake, 40 rolls of film of those events. Now we're talking about several thousand individual frames that were taken that the so-called authorities determined that you did not have a right to see. Oh, they were 'disruptive,' 'socially unacceptable,' 'politically unacceptable.' I've become furious. I'm a retired Command Sergeant Major. I was never famous for having a lot of patience."

In my own second book in the *Venus Rising* series, *Final Countdown: Rockets to Venus* (Terra Alta, West Virginia: Headline Books, 2017), I continue where Leonard left off and present you with more of the amazing United States and Soviet/Russian discoveries regarding the long-standing extraterrestrial presence on the Moon, especially with the Venusian colony Clarion on the hidden side that only a few select astronauts and contactees have enjoyed the privilege of seeing.

Acknowledgements

Over my fifty-three year history of investigating the flying saucers and exploring the mysteries of the Omniverse, there are literally thousands of friends, Earthlings and extraterrestrials, that have assisted me along the way- so many that a volume as large as a metropolitan telephone directory would be needed just to list them all.

Even so, I am extending a personal thank you to the following individuals for their kind assistance in the production of this book, ***The Vast Venus Conspiracy: Book IV in the Venus Rising: A Concise History of the Second Planet Series***, Kelly Bowman of the Gift of Light Expos in Columbus, Ohio; Ladies Aurora and Columba of Venus; Krsanna Duran, designer of the Time Star inter-dimensional model in Morgantown, West Virginia; Shu Hai Guo and all of the Venus Community in Shandong, China; David Houchin of the Harrison County Public Library in Clarksburg, West Virginia; Jeff Hutchinson, a fellow Vietnam era veteran from Las Vegas, Nevada, and friend of both Valiant Thor and the late Rev. Frank Stranges, who put me in contact with many others in the Inner Circle and protection of the Venusian Ring of Fire; Michael La Riche of the Coast-to-Coast A.M. Northeast Ohio Discussion Groups; Barbara Jean Lindsey, host of the ***Cosmic Oracle*** podcast in Plumas Lake, California; Shari Lynn, creator of the cosmic healing discs, in Ashtabula, Ohio; Lou Manley and his family from Bruceton Mills, West Virginia; for help in sundry endeavors; Omnec Onec, the ambassador of Fifth Dimensional Venus; Queen Orda of Abejar (Venus); Robert Potter of the Promise Revealed in Mt. Shasta, California; Anthony Pugliese, vice president of the Paranormal Search group in Harrisburg, Pennsylvania and time travel authority; Cathy Teets, president of Headline Books in Terra Alta, West Virginia; and Ross Weidler, president of the Paranormal Search group in Harrisburg, Pennsylvania.

To these and countless other angels who have helped me along the way, eternal blessings in the illumination of Lady Venus.

—Dr. Raymond A. Keller, II
Morgantown, West Virginia
18 June 2019

Index

A

Abejar 78, 140
Adamski, George 22, 44, 45, 49, 50, 51, 54, 55, 58, 70, 79, 98, 99, 100, 109, 111, 115, 121, 122, 123, 129, 133
Aerial Phenomena Research Organization (APRO) 36
Almaseda, Portugal 61
Amazing Stories 53, 99, 100, 101
American Federation of Labor 71
angel 12
Angel of the LORD 17
Anomaly 101
Apollo 11 129, 131, 134, 135, 136, 137
Argosy 59, 60, 130
Arnold, Doris 45, 46
Arnold, Kenneth 4, 34, 35, 39, 40, 41, 43, 44, 45, 46, 47, 49, 70, 104, 116
Articles of Faith 14
Astronomy 29, 126, 136
Aura Rhanes 58, 59, 60, 66, 77, 84, 94, 95, 96, 102

B

Baikonur Cosmodrome, Kazakhstan 25
balloon 24, 107
Barker, Gray 70, 81, 82, 83, 84, 94, 99, 100, 113, 114, 115, 116, 133
Barrios, Dolores, 6, 8, 53
Basa, Sidro L. 53, 54
Battlestar Galactica 18
Beckley, Timothy Green 46
Bender, Albert K. 81, 86, 105, 113
Bethurum, Truman 78, 79, 94
Bezymianny volcano 26
Bible 14, 15, 17, 58, 106
Bible Case for the UFO 106
Binder, Otto 73, 127, 128, 130, 134
bismuthinite 30
Black, John Q. 64
Blavatsky, Helena P. 35
blobs of light 40, 43, 44
Bloecher, Ted 55, 56, 64, 67
Book of Abraham 4, 11, 12, 13, 15, 16, 17, 18, 19
Book of Mormon 12
Borderland Sciences Research Association (BSRA) 47, 123
Buehler, Carl J. 45
Butte County, California 64, 65

C

Caerphilly Mountains, Wales 57
California Tourist Bureau 44
Call Air A-2 airplane 35
Cardiff, Wales 56
Cardoso, Cesar 61, 62
Cascade (s), mountain range, Washington State 35, 71, 104
Case for the UFO 106, 111
Catcher in the Rye 75
censorship 78, 79
Chandler, Michael 12
Chariots of the Gods 106
Chille, Frank 5, 6, 47, 48, 104
Ching Hai, Master 47
Christian 13, 17, 18, 38, 45
Christian Research Institute 13
Church of Jesus Christ of Latter-day Saints 11, 12, 13, 14, 16
Citizen-News, Los Angeles, California 66
Civilian Saucer Intelligence (CSI) 55, 64, 111, 112, 113
Clara John 59, 105
Clarion 58, 59, 60, 66, 77, 139
Clarke, Arthur C. 53
Cleveland Ufology Project (CUP) 82, 99
Cleveland UFO Society (CUFOS) 99
Cocoon 46
Coe, Albert 48, 49
Columbus of Space 32
comic book heroes 74
Community of Christ 11, 13, 14, 15, 18
Condon, Edward U. 119, 126, 132
Condon Report 123, 124, 125, 126, 127, 132, 133
contactee 5, 7, 8, 16, 40, 45, 47, 48, 58, 59, 62, 65, 66, 71, 79, 80, 82, 83, 84, 86, 87, 90, 94, 96, 99, 109, 111, 115, 121, 122, 123, 131, 132, 133
cosmic evolution 15, 17, 19
Cosmic Ray's Excellent Venus Adventure 7, 53, 60, 65, 94

D

Daily Mail, London, United Kingdom 30, 56
Daily News, New York City 71, 72, 78
Dante 34
Dean, Robert 125, 139
demythologizing 18, 19
denominations 19
Desert Center, California 1, 54, 98, 99
Diario De Lisboa, Lisbon, Portugal 61
disclosure 9, 21, 118, 134
Divine Comedy 34
Dixon, Jeane 58
Duran, Krsanna 65, 140

E

Edwards Air Force Base, California 99
Edwards, Frank 70, 71, 72, 128
Epitome of Faith and Doctrine 14
"Evening Star" 23
ex-nihilo 12
Exopolitics Summit, Barcelona, Spain 139

F

Federal Communications Commission 78
Filer, George 104
Final Countdown: Rockets to Venus 22, 46, 74, 83, 98, 139
Flatwoods Monster 81, 114
"Fly Fishing Venusian" 48
Flying Saucer Conspiracy 45
Flying Saucer Party 77
Flying Saucers Farewell 51
Flying Saucers Have Landed 45, 54, 111
Fodor, Nodor 74
Forster, Irene 88, 89
Forster, Jack 86, 87, 88

G

Galaxy 92
"Galaxy Being" 92
galena 30
Garrett, Dixie 65
Genesis 15
Giant Rock, Landers, California 65, 66, 70, 98
Girl on the Rock 115
Gnostic 11, 12, 17, 54
gods 12, 13, 14, 15, 16, 17, 18, 19, 23, 85, 122
Gospel of Judas 54
Gray Barker Collection 70, 94
Green, Gabriel 5, 6, 46, 77, 111
Grinspoon, David 21
Gross, Ben 71, 72, 73, 74, 78, 79

H

Heinlein, Robert A. 18
higher dimensional planes 19
Hotel Woodstock, New York City 82
Houston, Texas 26, 27, 29
Hynek, J. Allen 7, 22, 119, 123, 124, 125, 134, 135, 136

I

Inquirer, Philadelphia, Pennsylvania 131
International Flying Saucer Bureau (IFSB) 81, 86, 105, 113
Interplanetary Spacecraft Convention 59, 66, 84, 96, 98
Invaders, The 62
Izvestiya, Soviet Union 129

J

Jefferson, Thomas 68
Jessup, Morris K 106, 111, 128
Jesus Christ 11, 12, 13, 14, 16, 17, 18, 38, 45
Jet Propulsion Laboratory (JPL) 24, 25, 29, 130, 131, 139
Jupiter 66

K

Keel, John A. Keel 22, 47, 101, 102, 133
Keller, Raymond A. 1, 2, 5, 10, 11, 17, 23, 34, 35, 36, 47, 48, 53, 57, 65, 66, 71, 73, 78, 81, 86, 96, 98, 99, 100, 112, 122, 131, 140
Kennedy, John F. 129
Keyhoe, Donald E. 36, 45, 111, 133
Knight, Kitty 45
Knight, Oscar 42, 44, 45
"Kor, Peter" 98, 99, 100
Ksanfomaliti, Leonid 32

L

Lady Aurora 10, 78
Lady Columba 10, 78
Lady Gaga 26, 32, 33
Lady Selene 37, 38, 40
Lady Venus 85, 140
Lake Trout, Ontario, Canada 48
LaRiche, Michael A. 82, 99, 100
Larson, Glen A. 18
Last Temptation of Christ 75
Layne, Meade 47, 84, 122, 123
"lens cap" 28
Life on Other Planets 35
Light of Understanding 62
Lithbridge, Joshua 56, 57
Little Listening Post 59, 69, 70, 71, 77, 105
Lorenzen, Jim 36

M

Magellan 29
Marcattilio, Pat 104
maria 138
Master of the World, The 56
Masursky 26, 27

Maxwell Montes 30, 31
McDonald, James E. 4, 82, 83, 117, 118, 119, 120, 121, 122, 123, 124, 125, 126, 127, 128
Menger, Connie and Howard 22, 47, 59, 71, 73, 74, 79, 84, 114, 115, 129, 131, 132, 133
Men in Black 81, 82, 133
Michael 12, 17, 22, 82, 83, 99, 100, 140
Miracle on 34th Street 74
Mirror, London, United Kingdom 50, 51
Mofjell, Norway 60
Mormon Boundary 13, 16
Morning Call, Allentown, Pennsylvania 131
"Morning Star" 23
Moseley, James 82, 83, 89
Mothman 81
MQ707 99
Mr. Smith Goes to Washington 77
Mt. Shasta 5, 9, 47, 48, 65, 99, 140
MUFON 49, 50, 51
Munsick, Lee 104, 105, 106, 107, 108, 109, 110, 111, 112, 113, 114, 115, 116
Mutual Broadcasting Company 70, 71, 86
Mutual Broadcasting Corporation 78, 79
Mutual UFO Network (MUFON) 49, 51, 125

N

National Aeronautics and Space Administration (NASA) 7, 21, 22, 26, 27, 29, 30, 31, 64, 120, 129, 130, 131, 137, 138, 139
National Geographic 137
National Investigations Committee on Aerial Phenomena (NICAP) 36, 55, 105, 106, 107, 110, 111, 113, 124
National Press Club 58
National UFO Reporting Center 63
Native Americans 12, 23
Nebel, Long John 4, 66, 68, 69, 70, 71, 72, 73, 74, 75, 76, 77, 78, 79, 80, 82, 84, 86
Nelson, Buck 78
Nephites 12
Ness, Eliot 82
New Testament 15, 77
Nexus 82, 85, 89, 98, 133
Nightbeat 78
nimbus 8, 74
Nixon, Richard M. 134, 135, 136
"North Coast Mike" 82, 83, 84, 90
Northwestern University 22, 119, 134, 136
nudism 36, 116
nudists 45, 49

O

Omnec Onec 8, 47, 140
Orthon 54, 55, 98, 100, 122
Outer Limits 92

P

Palmer, Raymond A. 53, 54, 99, 100, 101, 102, 133
Paradise, California 35, 65
Paradise Interplanetary Space-Craft Club 65
Party Line 68, 69, 70, 71, 72, 75, 76, 77, 78, 79, 80, 84, 86
Paterson News, New Jersey 130
Pen and Pencil, New York City 72
PJ Media 62
Pleroma 8, 17
Pluto 66
Pontius Pilate 75
postage stamp 24
Potter, Rob 4, 5, 9, 47, 48, 84, 99, 140
Private Dancer 103
Project Bluebook 22, 110, 111

Q

Queen Orda 7, 8, 10, 78, 140
Quinn Martin Productions 62
Quorum of the Twelve Apostles 16

R

Ramirez, Joe 66, 67
Reeve, Bryant 109
religion 14, 17, 18, 38, 122
Rense, Jeff 131, 132
Reorganized Church of Jesus Christ of Latter Day Saints 11, 13, 14, 16, 18
"re-symbolization" 18
Roberts, August C. 73, 81, 82, 131, 132, 133, 134
Roman Empire 84, 85
Rowe, Kevin 66
Royal Order of Tibet 51
Rubio, Mark O. 64
Rumi, Jalal ad-Din Muhammad 34
Ryan Aeronautical Company 110

S

Saucerian, The 81, 83, 84, 99, 114, 115, 116, 132, 133
Saucer News 82, 89
Schmidt, J. E. 78, 79
science fiction 18, 30, 32, 46, 57, 62, 72, 101, 102, 114, 133, 134
Scientific Study of Unidentified Flying Objects 119, 123, 133
scorpion 26, 32

Serviss, Garrett 32
Seventh-Day Adventist Church 58
Sierra Nevada 41
skinny dipping 45
Smith, Evelyn 59, 102
Smith, III, Joseph 14, 15, 16
Snow, Lorenzo 15, 16, 19
Solar System Research 32
Solvang, Aasta 60
Somebody Else Is on the Moon 137, 138, 139
"Space Girl" 4, 81, 84, 87, 88, 89, 94
Spartacus 95, 102
spectroscopy 24, 29
Starship Troopers 18
Star Trek: The Next Generation 83
Stranger in the Pentagon 132
Stranges, Frank 8, 62, 132, 140
Stryk, Ted 28
"Super Spectrum" 101
Swedenborg, Emanuel 17, 35

T

technology 6, 8, 39, 64, 67, 77, 85, 87, 95, 111, 117, 118, 119, 122
teleportation 72, 73, 74
temperature 24, 25, 26, 31, 38, 107
Tesla, Nikola 98
Theophanic Angel 17
Thinnes, Roy 62
Thompson, Samuel Eaton 34, 36, 37, 38, 39, 40
Tibetan Buddhism 38
Time Machine, The 57
Times and Seasons 14
Times Register, Bedford, Ohio 83
topography 29
Turner, Tina 103

U

UFO Review 46
Union of Soviet Socialist Republics (USSR) 23, 25, 55, 76
United Press International 22, 26, 131
United States Geological Survey 26, 27

V

Valiant Thor 62, 132, 140
Valor: The Magazine of Soulcraft 98
Van Tassel, George 65, 70
vegetarians 38
Venera 13 24, 26, 27, 28, 32
Venera 14 24, 25, 26, 27
Venusian "Horseman" 1, 4, 6, 8, 9, 22, 24, 25, 26, 27, 28, 30, 31, 34, 37, 40, 42, 45, 46, 47, 48, 49, 51, 53, 54, 58, 59, 60, 61, 62, 63, 65, 66, 70, 74, 77, 78, 81, 84, 85, 96, 98, 102, 114, 115, 116, 124, 129, 131, 132, 139, 140
Venus Rising: A Concise History of the Second Planet, see also Keller, Raymond A. 17, 54, 115, 140
Verne, Jules 56
Viking 1 136
von Däniken, Erich 11, 106

W

water 21, 22, 23, 25, 27, 29, 30, 35, 37, 40, 42, 49, 53, 64, 65, 95, 138
Welch, Tahnee 46
Wells, H. G. 57
Whalen, Zara 50
Wiessmann, Joan 131, 132, 133
Williamson, George Hunt 1, 98, 99, 100
Wingate, John 78
Wizard of Oz 75
Wolverton Meadow, California 41
Wolverton Trail, California 40, 41
WOR, New York City 66, 68, 69, 70, 71, 72, 79, 84, 86
World Telegram and Sun, New York City 64
WZAK, Cleveland, Ohio 82, 83

Y

Young, Brigham 14, 15, 18, 19

Z

Zimmerman, John 68
Zret 49